Success Lockdown:
Life After Incarceration

By Dr. Tori Brown

Published By

Success Lockdown Group LLC

Tampa, Florida

Success Lockdown: Life After Incarceration

Copyright © 2022 by Dr. Tori Brown

All rights reserved. Printed in The United States of America. No part of this publication may be reproduced, stored in a retrieval system or transmitted in any form or by any means electronic, mechanical, photography, copying, recording or otherwise, without prior written permission of the publisher, except in the case of brief quotations embodied in critical articles and reviews. The author rights to "freedom speech' protected by and with the 1st Amendment of the constitution of the United States of America. Books may be purchased for educational, business, or sales promotional use. For information please email successlockdown@gmail.com.

Published in the United States by Success Lockdown Group LLC

Located in Tampa Florida

ISBN: 978-1-7351332-9-4 (Print)

ISBN: 978-0-578-29729-3 (E Book)

Library of Congress Control Number: 2022937481

First Edition

Table of Contents

Dedication 1

Preface 2

Introduction 3

Ch 1:   Exposure 7

Ch 2:   Getting Back out into the World 13

Ch 3:   Getting Down to Business 21

Ch 4:   Starting the Business 29

Ch 5:   Credit to Your Race 38

Ch 6:   Business Operations 47

Ch 7:   Business Operations (Part 2) 56

Ch 8:   Building Business Funding and Growing Business Assets 65

Ch 9:   The Importance of Self Promotion and Networking in Business .. 75

Ch 10: Success Lockdown 82

Dedication

I dedicate this book to the ones that have a voice but have not found the courage to write it down. I will speak for you today, but tomorrow you must speak for us all (felons).

- Dr. Tori Brown

Dearest Juanita Brown, Mommy I love you like a lion, yet I was born a Taurus and will forever be stubborn about mine.

John Thomas Brown (Dad), you are gone but not gone away. I look in the mirror and I see you in my frown, my smile, as my nostrils flair only to realize that you will always be there.

To Pearlie Oglesby and Claude Oglesby, I am an extension of your intellect, care, strength, and greatness. Grandparents like you raise children to become the light for the world to see.

To Buelah and John Brown my paternal grandparents, you are my love. I did not know you well, but I loved you for my creation through lineage. I hope to represent you well.

To Buelah Harmon my dearest aunt, you have loved me unconditionally all my life for that I am forever grateful. To aunt Sallie Martin, your prayers and encouragement still continues to carry me in 2022. Thank you!

Special thanks to Dr. Leona Allen you are a lifesaver gifted and ordained. Thank you!

I am dedicating these pages to my friends, family, and supporters. Special dedication to Taja Grimes (Green) friend for life, Angelis Beavers, George Johnson, Corves T. Wright, Camilyah Johnson Buxton, Tiffany Rachann and my publisher My Mommy! Love is without sayings, words are without void, life is without choices, may I carry your heavy load in my work and impact!

Preface

Although I have only known Dr. Tori Brown for a short period of time, our immediate connection has made it feel like a lifetime. She is one of the smartest, most ambitious, and most caring people I have ever met, and that's why I am drawn to her.

From our very first encounter, I knew she was someone who would change the lives of many people. It was a goal we shared in common. Like myself, she saw the inequities in our society and wanted to do something about it.

When she trusted me with her story, I didn't see an ex-felon, I saw the American dream at its best. I saw a beautiful woman who made a mistake, paid for her mistake, and refused to let society keep making her pay for it. I saw a beautiful woman who had more power than she realized, an anointing that put her in a special place to do God's work. I saw a beautiful woman who needed to heal from a mistake that happened two decades ago, and use that healing to deliver others so that from their mistakes, they too could Lockdown Success as well.

I went to law school to help people from a legal standpoint, but Dr. Brown has all the capabilities of helping them from a business standpoint. She didn't write this book to make a profit, she wrote this book to make a difference. I am glad to be a part of this difference, and hope that it makes a difference in your life, the same way meeting her, and knowing her, has made a difference in mine.

Read her story, take her advice, and find greatness within yourself the same way she did! I wish you luck on the road to Success Lockdown!

Warmest Regards,

Cassandra Henderson, ESQ

Introduction

I didn't always want to be a business owner. Things just went that way because of the set of circumstances that were being experienced in my life. Fresh out of jail with a college degree and one year of graduate school. How in the hell did that happen right? I ask myself that often until the memory of waking up out of a dream from being incarcerated all night reminds me. "Yes that is true." To this day, I still have bad dreams about the year spent in county jail for serving out my one-year sentence in Michigan in 1999. Do you remember the song "1999" by Prince when it came out back in 1982? I do, in fact my siblings and I would play it and ask ourselves, "What do you think we will be doing by the time 1999 comes?" I sure in the heck did not anticipate jail time. I was charged with the crime in 1996 but did not get sentenced until 1998. Dealing with one wrong turn in my life cost me 10 years or more of my life. 10 years? "Yes" … but how? Let's calculate this together. Let's do the math.

Year one was the crime. I admit there were problems going on in my life. I was angry at the world. The pain of life itself at an early age was manifesting in my criminal lifestyle of selling drugs and gang activity. At the time, it was a way of life. I didn't have to have it. I wanted to be included. That's my truth. I wanted to be rich. That was my nemesis at that time. I wanted to be influential with my gift of organization and management. What better way than to use those skills than to distribute marijuana in my community. I didn't give a damn about community and the impact my sales were having in that place everyone was calling community. My community was filled with crack rocks, guns, and pimps. What was so important about community at the time? My environment did not seem like it was making any impact on me that allowed me to matter. So I had to ask myself why in the world do I give a fuck about community. What has the community done for me?

Here is what leads to year two: the wait time. I was going to court almost every month it seemed. All these fancy words being thrown at me by the attorney. Adjudication, incarceration, filing a motion, deposition, character witness. I was so confused. All I heard was that for one wrong turn in my life I was facing 3 to 15 years in prison. At the time I was a student in college working on my bachelor's degree in psychology. My goals were being pulled from right under me at a blink of an eye. Depression was starting to set in. Anxiety attacks were beginning to start. I didn't know what that was. I thought I was having a heart attack. Dying on my feet. Every day when I would look in the mirror my face was unrecognizable.

The stress was putting more weight on my body than I needed, and chest pains were starting to increase. The next thing I remember is being at a doctor's appointment weighing 350 pounds and being diagnosed with high blood pressure. No shit Sherlock. I'm going to jail like my lawyer said. But her job would be to minimize the time I would go. Did this bitch just give me my jail sentence? Did I pay her to be my fucking judge and jury? I guess so. Officially depressed and staying in my bed more than I needed to was my year two and three as I awaited my trial date from my college dormitory. Suicide is real in the mind of the lost. I was not planning suicide but I did have ideations.

My friends did not recognize me. I was slipping away right before their eyes. Sentenced in year three was hell and hot water at the same time. I found a walk with God at the time. They say once you get in trouble like this the first thing you do is call on Jesus. "Yes" I am not ashamed of that. I did call him because I really needed him. I had to make sense of my life and its existence. If it had not been for my walk with Christ, life would have not been the same. At the end of the day that is the strongest thing I ever have going for me in my favor. Year four was my time spent in the county jail. According to my attorney I was supposed to turn myself into jail and she would get me a court date within the week to challenge the sentence. Apparently the wording in my sentence read, "Report to jail immediately after graduation." It did not specify graduation of what or when. So the argument would be that I was currently enrolled in my first year of graduate school at the university pursuing a Master's Degree in Community Counseling. (There goes that word community again) Again, this attorney said report to jail on new year's eve of 1998 and you will be out of there and back in school for winter semester of 1999. Wrong information.

I sat there in the jail cell waiting on them to call my name. I told myself that I didn't have to eat that food in there because by the time I get really hungry they will be calling my name to leave. It did not happen. I sat for a year without an out date in their jail computer system. I did the time and I lost the weight while doing the time. Year five and I am out and back in population. We called it, "back in the world". I felt like Tupac Shakur my favorite rapper. I was hungry for life. I needed to find some completion. I needed guidance. I was still having anxiety attacks. I was still depressed. I did not talk much. I did not watch television anymore. I did not eat meat. I did not trust anyone. I sure in the hell did not trust the law. I hated lawyers and cursed their name. Do not talk to me. I was not taking any college courses on criminal justice ever. I was different. I was hurting. I was wounded. I was emotional inside. I could not sleep through the night in the dark. I had incarceration behavior. Most hideously, I had two felons that prohibited me from getting employment. They even told me that I couldn't even vote. What I did have, was a bachelor's degree and almost ready to complete my Master's Degree. I worked very hard to educate myself and dedicate myself to helping others.

Year six I had a graduate degree in counseling. I had a degree and I still had depression and suicidal ideations. I learned how to minimize those thoughts through my relationship with Christ. I Tried to take my felonies and degrees and get a job. Don't make you laugh right? You guessed it. Not interested. No one wanted to hire a felon with two degrees. My heart was broken. Dr. Tina Parkman was my blessing. She was introduced to me by my credit man. Yes I had a credit man. A credit man was this guy that discovered fraud on my credit report that occurred during my time of incarceration. He removed all the derogatory items from my credit report to improve my credit score. Yes, my credit man introduced me to her. She spoke words of encouragement in my life to strip me of all of the barriers that were holding me back from my success. She spoke entrepreneurship into my life. Year seven I became a business owner. I get it…I will hire myself. I will start a business that will help the lost that look just like me. They think like me, they act like me, hell they are me, they are felons.

I did get hired eventually for $22K a year. With a first year second graduate degree student I thought things would get better. It did for a while until the dreams started. I would have this recurring dream that I would visit someone in jail and they would mistake me for an inmate and lock me up. Waking up in tears hollering, "I'm innocent, I'm not supposed to be here". Those nights were the worst. Year eight was good because I felt like there was light at the end of my tunnel. I was a business owner and even managed to get accepted in a PHD Program after I completed my second Master's Degree in School Counseling. Everything was good except $22k a year living downtown Detroit was not getting all of the bills paid. I needed more income so I went into counsel with Dr. Tina and she challenged me to do more with the business that I started.

Year nine was full of enlightenment. Yet still having bad dreams about jail. Still getting rejected for better employment. Still not able to vote. I learned a new word for the 2008, disenfranchised voter right. Rights? I had rights? What are rights? Sure I heard of the Civil Rights Movement. Even heard on the show cops, "You have the right to remain silent." But what in the world happened to my voting rights. You mean I lost them and can't get them back. So when I was voting all of those times my vote did not matter. See one thing that my parents instilled in me early is that people died because black people could not vote. So I rather believed in the voting process or my vote being counted or not. " I better have my black ass at the poles, come voting day" I quote them. I did, ye, come to find out, my vote was not even being counted. Imagine that.

Year ten was transitional. I was still dealing with depression. I could not find another employment opportunity. I was stuck yet I still had a business. See those were ten years that I felt like I lost. Young women my age were living their life. My friends were getting married and most had children. They had families and careers. I had felonies, fears, reservations, and trust issues.

Chapter 1:
Exposure

I wanted to start this book project by number one saying it's a project. I never thought I would be at a place to write something like this because of being convicted of felonies and talking about it, especially in a public project like this. I never thought that this would be something that I would do. But I do this today because I realize that there are so many people that are dependent on people like me to talk about my experiences in order to expose a population of people who have never had an opportunity to understand what it's like to be a felon. And to help people understand it is not an easy position to do time, experience incarceration and then come out and be successful.

There were so many things that I had going for myself. I was in undergrad when I got convicted and charged with my felony. But I also had a lot of strikes against me. You know, I'm a first generation college student. I am a first generation of legal business ownership. And I'm the first to do time in jail in my family. Those are diverse firsts, right? I'm not proud of it. The only thing that I can be proud of is my approach to dealing with this. I'm not proud of what I had to do. I'm not proud of how I did it. But I am proud of the way I positioned myself to come back. My plan was important. My purpose is very important.

Doing time does a lot to you mentally. It changes you. It gives you nights of hopelessness. Days of frustration. It gives you hidden shame from being a felon. The way I connect with people, even twenty years later, it's different because of my experiences being incarceration. There's not a day that I'm not driving in my car, that I own, that I paid for. I'm licensed and I'm insured but then when that cop car gets behind me I get nervous. I get nervous as hell. I know that I ain't even done nothin' but what if I got a bench warrant and I'm not aware of? What if someone accuse me of doing something that I didn't do? See once you're a felon, you are always the guilty party in your mind. The guilty party that did it. If anybody did it, you did it. It's like that movie, about the murder on the orient express, I haven't seen the movie, so I can't use it for a strong reference, but I can imagine that the movie is about a murder that occurs on the train right, and they're trying to find out who's the like candidate that did it. If there's eight or nine people on that train and everybody has different backgrounds, you can believe if there's a felon on that train all them arrows goin' to point at that felon for that murder.

So that fear, even after the fact, twenty years later that fear is always there. Some days I forget I'm a felon and then there's a friendly reminder. It could be something on the news where a successful politician didn't disclose he had a run in with the law, years before his political seat. And those spear campaigns get to talking about it and man, I just shake my head 'cause, I'm like "wow, that's hard you know. There are so many things that make your life after incarceration difficult.

As I mentioned before, those who know me, know I don't eat meat. And I stopped eating it in jail, of course. I was out the other day with a friend and we were at IHOP eating pancakes. She doesn't eat syrup. Now she had her reason why she doesn't eat syrup, I have my reasons why I don't eat syrup. In jail there was no syrup. Syrup was a special occasion. If the jail had syrup, we was on top of the world that week. So I didn't get used to having syrup on my pancakes because there was no expectations to have syrup. The guard would remind us over and over again "Bitch you in jail!" Even down to the point of asking for some maxi pads. "Bitch you in jail!" But Ma'am I'm a heavy bleeder. She didn't care, you were in jail. So you think I was going to complain about not having syrup if I can't even have maxi pads? So no, to this day, I don't eat syrup. I never got my mind used to having syrup again. In fact, I try not to buy it. Twenty years ago, something happened and I still don't eat syrup.

I don't eat salt. Salt was another thing in "there" for special occasions, so to this day, I don't eat salt. I don't buy it. I have to buy it for my mother, she wants it. In fact, throughout my health recovery, I had to buy pink salt per my doctor's instructions. To increase something in my body. So there's occasions where I salt my food now, or season it when I cook it with pink salt. But that took adjustment, to buy salt. It did. So there's things that I experience every day twenty years later, aside from the dreams. Things that continue to put me in the mindset of why this book is important. And the mindset that this isn't just about being a book. It's a project. I have to help people understand that it's not easy for a felon to come out of an incarceration and mainstream normally. It's not easy to connect to people. It's not easy to relate to people. I was in a dormitory with all ladies from different social and economic backgrounds and different ethnic groups. I learned how to braid hair, french braid hair, during my lockdown time.

I learned how to make "jail macaroni and cheese," yes there are jail recipes for those who don't know. When you are there, you learn how to make jail cuisine. If I don't see another cup of Ramen Noodles, I'll be okay. To this day I will run past the Ramen Noodles in the grocery store. I hate Ramen Noodles. I do not like them. That was a part of commissary and I bought a lot of Ramen Noodles. I refuse to eat a Ramen Noodle today. I learned while in there to make this Ramen Noodle Macaroni and Cheese. We didn't have macaroni and cheese so we had to make our own. What we would do is take cheetos and crush them up in the bag and dump them into the Ramen Noodle cup; and if you got really fancy you added some squeeze cheese in there; and for those who ate meat, you would cut up some sausages and put that in there too as well; you would microwave that baby on high and you got macaroni and cheese courtesy of commissary. That is jail cuisine at its finest. I ate beans and I would season the beans with mustard packets. That was my seasoning on my food. I would have bologna sandwiches. Sometimes they would give us paper bag sandwiches and I would have bologna sandwiches and I would take the meat out of there and just eat bread and the mayonnaise, squeeze a little mustard on it and I had instant jail cuisine.

There were a lot of things that I learned while I sat there during my time. I learned how to get to know myself better. Meaning, when I was told that I had to do that urine sometime in jail, I didn't think I could do it. I thought that I would lose my mind literally. I didn't realize that I would learn how to adapt to my environment as quickly as I did. After I realized that they were not going to let me out of there, I had to learn how to depend on my inner strength. I had to pray a lot. I had to seek everything within me to try to find something to survive for. Remember I still had the pressure. Remember I still had suicidal ideation. Remember I still was feeling hopeless. I had to find some hope. I had to find a reason to exist in that environment.

Sitting there, I got a chance to get to know some very interesting young ladies. And I learned their story and how they got there and I learned to be an individual amidst the other individuals in that environment. Some were mothers, some were wives, some were even here from another country and they got caught up into something criminally and had to do time. Some were crackheads, some were church leaders, some were people who were passing through. They might have had a DUI for drunk driving, some may have killed their child, but no matter what the reason they were in there for, I began to see that they all had a reason to get to that next day. And I had to learn to find a reason to get to that next day 'cause I knew if I could get to the next day I could get to the next day after that and I could get to the next day after that. So I really learned to take it day by day. I felt mentally I was losing time. But at the same time, I was learning how to balance my mind and keep my wits.

My mom would send me books that I would read. I remember writing a letter to Creflo Dollar, the preacher, and low and behold, I don't know if it was him, himself or his staff, but they wrote back. And every week that ministry would send me something that would get me through another week. Now people talk bad about Television Evangelists and preachers and some of them, their suspicions may be correct. But at that time in my life, that time and that season in my life, Creflo Dollar wrote back to me, his ministry, they wrote back. They gave me words of encouragement, they gave me words of life. And that helped me.

Another thing that helped me was an older lady, we called her the Church Lady. She would come in and give you stamps, and cards and just things to let you know somebody was thinking of you. And she would come and she would talk to you. And pray for you and pray with you. And she would even reach out to your loved ones if you needed her to. I remember when I had her reach out to mine. It was during the time when my mom had suffered a stroke while I was in jail. And I was very distraught that I couldn't be there. I was very distraught because I couldn't be there for my granny. My grandmother was in a nursing home at the time. And she was the last face that I had seen before I went into jail and they dropped me off. My grandmother has always meant a lot to me. Out of all of the people in my life, she's always been the most unapologetic supporter in my life. I mean unapologetically, she would never apologize for supporting me during my incarceration period. She knew I was going to be gone for a while. But she knew that it was important for me to come back. And she expressed that since I was back, I was ordered, and she would tell me, "That's an Order!" You are ordered to do something strong and positive. It's 2017 about to be 2018 and grandmother, this project is strong and positive. I miss her a lot. I have a lot of her in me and I thank God for it.

During that time, I kept my mind on my grandmother, my mother, my father, my sister and my brother, and my family. I kept my mind on what I would be when I get out of here. I kept my mind on the impact that I would make. During the same time I was in jail, a good friend, best friend, boyfriend, everything to me, Derrick, he was locked up too. He wrote to me often, and I wrote him back often. I appreciated the companionship through my incarceration time from him. Even in incarceration he continued to be a companion. He's locked up now for mandatory life. And I hate it. I miss my best friend that I have known for my almost whole young life. Derrick was my best friend. He knew everything about me. He knew all of my secrets. He knew all about my thoughts and how I would feel. I was inspired by Derrick when I left jail, 1. to never return but 2. Do something for people like "us" he said. I'm doing everything I can on the outside to represent those on the inside. It hurts me a lot sometimes and I often feel like I should do more. But at this season in my life, I'm telling a story to encourage others that as they read this book, they may understand that they are not alone. That people like me didn't forget that they have felonies because I can't forget. I can't forget the sound of the jail door closing. To this day, I hate to visit people in jail 'cause I hate that sound. I hate being with the thought that when that door closes, it's so permanent. It's kind of like when they lower the casket down at a funeral. It's so permanent. It's the same feeling if you ain't never felt that before. You don't know. You may have felt how you feel when they lower your loved one down in that casket. That happens one time, right? But imagine when you go from visitation to visiting someone who's coming to jail to see you. And then when that hour is done, you have to go back to your cell and that door closes. It's just as permanent. My mother came to visit me behind the glass twice a week. There was only one week that my mother missed, and that was the week she had a stroke. My brother's girlfriend at the time, God bless her soul, another influencer in my life Angelis Beavers, came and she visited me. I just want to say one thing about Angelis, though she died of cancer, it looked like she lost but she won. Even in her death, she won. Angelis influenced me to dream, even after my jail time. She was one of my contributors to helping me start my business. She was on my Board of Directors. She was my accountability for finances. She was my fiscal rock. She was my sister. I miss her and I love her. But she's not forgotten 'cause she is not gone. And that's what this is all about. Doing something that's lasting. So whatever you do in life. You're not forgotten. You're not gone. The legacy of what you do should last forever.

    Success Lockdown, I dedicate this to YOU, the one who picked up this book because I want you to be successful. I want you to have the tools you need to rise above adversity that was put in your path. I want you to see that you matter. I want you to know that despite everything that you have been through, you deserve to Lockdown Success. So I give you Success Lockdown with love, honor, admiration, and hope that your future is going to be 1000 times better than the past you had to experience. This is my blessing and decree for you.

Chapter 2:
Getting Back out into the World

    I remember waking up that morning. You never know when you're out date is coming. As I mentioned before, I didn't even have an out date in the computer system. No one knew when I was getting out. I knew that I had written the judge every week from the time I was incarcerated. I figured if I just write him every week and plead my case, I could wear him down. I read it somewhere in the bible about a lady who continued to petition the judge in the bible regarding her children and the judge got worn down to move in her favor. I read the word of God and I believe it. I apply it to myself every chance I get. So, I had nothing to do but sit there in that cell so I wrote the judge every week. And wouldn't you know, just like the bible verse that speaks about it, they actually let me out a week early to attend my father's retirement party. They released me on an electronic tether device. But I still got out early. So here I am, waiting, and didn't know which day they were going to let me out early. I did get word back that they were planning to release me early.

    So here I am laying in the cell and the lady comes around to get my urine. She says that I have to take this urine test to make sure that I didn't smoke any marijuana or do any drugs while I was there. I know I hadn't smoked any marijuana. I know I didn't do any drugs but I was so damn nervous to pee. And besides I didn't have to pee. She told me that if I did not pee now, she would not come back until tomorrow because that was the rule. So I had to go and pee. While I was sitting there in the bathroom trying to pee and give this lady urine, all kinds of stuff was going through my head. (*Was I around anyone that smoked any marijuana? Could somebody contaminate my urine and make it seem like I was on drugs?*) I was in fear. I was afraid something was going to jeopardize my opportunity to leave out that day. But, just like my grandmother would say, "Did you make water yet?" That's what my grandmother would say when she actually got to go to the bathroom. She was from Twin City, Georgia, backwoods. So yes, I made water. Gave her the urine, next thing

I know, I'm packing up everything and I'm leaving.

I can remember it to this day, walking down that dark corridor. See, when you're in lockdown. The dormitory for girls or women. You are in the dark for most of the period of your time there. I don't know if they mean to do that on purpose or not. So for a year, I did not see actual daylight. There was no fresh sunshine on my face. We did not have an opportunity to exercise. Men could go and work out and exercise. Women, we didn't have that opportunity in County Jail. We had to stay in, pretty much exercise on our own.

So there I am, walking towards daylight, walking towards sunshine, it's dark. Clothes falling off of me, I had lost a lot of weight in jail. I could have done a jail weight loss commercial. I often teased myself after being released. I remember holding my pants, holding my garbage bag sack of commissary clothes I had accumulated over the year, my bible, my books, my drawings, everything that I had accumulated. I put it right over my shoulder and I'm running. I didn't even know if they had called my parents to pick me up. I didn't care. All I know is, they said I can go and I was ready to go. I was escorted out by Frank. Mr. Frank was a good guard. He was happy to see me leave and I was happy to be going. As I was walking, I started running towards the light. I was free. I was finally free. I ran out into the streets. And it was the beautiful sun that I saw, it was just very beautiful. I mean, the dirty streets of Saginaw, Michigan, though they were still dirty, it was a beautiful dirty to me, because I hadn't seen them for over a year. I kissed the sidewalk. Yeah, I did. People say that's cliche when you get out, but no, that was real for me. I bent down, and I kissed that nasty, dirty sidewalk 'cause I was free.

As I'm walking, I don't even know where I am walking to. All I know is I need to figure out which direction is home. So, I'm just running towards Michigan Ave. I knew Michigan Ave could get me somewhere closer to home. I didn't know if I was going to find a pay phone, someone that I could use their phone. I don't know, I was just trying to get out of there. I heard a horn blowing and I looked, there goes my dad driving the cadillac. I hadn't seen my dad in a whole year. My dad wouldn't come see me in jail. He just refused to see me like that. At the time I didn't understand it, but now growing up being an adult and he's passed on now. I get it. Nobody wants to see their baby girl in lockdown. He could handle a lot of things because my dad is a strong man. He was a strong man. He's deceased now, 2012. He's my superman. But one thing superman can't stand is the kryptonite of his baby girl wrongly put in jail for something that she shouldn't have been put in jail for. Should I have been punished? Absolutely. Should I have gotten time? Absolutely not. Superman had his kryptonite, his baby girl doing jail time. He refused to come visit me. But my mother on the other hand, she's the real champ.

Several strokes by this time in her life, yet she still made it her business to be there for me. She would come visit me every week, in fact twice a week. I had visitations twice a week and I had her there twice a week coming to see me. Some days she didn't even feel good. Some days she didn't even want to see me through that glass. Some days I didn't even want to see her through that glass. I felt like I had failed her. I remember my favorite rapper Tupak Shakur saying:

"I reminisce on the stress I caused, it was hell Hugging' on my mama from a jail cell And who'd think in elementary? Hey! I see the penitentiary.

Those words I heard them when the hit first came out by Tupak, never thought that would be a reality of mine.

My mom, my dad were in the car and they were so glad to see me they stopped in the middle of the street. Held up traffic and hugged me. My dad hadn't seen me, he picked me up. He could pick me up now, I was no longer 300 lbs. I was more like 200, he was a strong man, he could handle 300 or 200. He's my dad, he will always be able to pick me up. That's what he said. As a child, he called me his Roots baby and raised me up to the sky from his bed. As a grown adult, I was always his Roots baby so he will always be able to lift me up. Standing there in the road looking at my parents ready to get in that car in case somebody got ready to change that mind about me going back to jail. I don't know, I had this paranoia that something was going to send me back that minute.

God, that's the worst, those dreams I have, they are the worst. I had to write this book because I wanted to confront the worst. I needed to confront the worst. I needed to write this book because I wanted someone who has experienced what I have experienced to know that you are not the only one to feel like you do. I know I'm not the only one that feels like I do about this whole entire thing. I want this book to be a resource for those getting' back in the world. Because getting' back in the world is not always easy.

The truth is sometimes people don't have people to come pick them up. They are sent off and they have nothing. Thank God I had my parents. They picked me up. They took me home. But then there is that transition I had to deal with. Getting back in the world. That's not always an easy feat. It wasn't easy for me, even with a college degree and a first year graduate student. It still wasn't easy for me. I had to plan prior to me leaving jail. I had to plan for success before I left. I had to devise a strategy before I left those cells. The best way to deal with adversity is to plan success. As I sat in those jail cells and I thought, "What am I going to do on my release date, whenever that release date comes, What is it going to be like on my release date? How do I punch back? Because I definitely got knocked out. I got knocked the hell out. I'm in jail. But I'm going to punch back. I'm going to block and I'm going to punch. I have never been a street fighter or nothin' like that. But I had enough common sense to know that when somebody hit you, or something in life hit you, you better punch it back. And that's what I was doing' sitting in those jail cell punching. My mind was punching, my soul was punching, my punch was punching. I was punching back.

My last few months prior to getting out, I actually wrote from commissary paper and commissary pencil, I wrote a letter to my advisor, Dr. Calloway at Eastern Michigan University. I wrote to her and let her know that the reason I had taken time out is because I had to spend a year in jail. When I left, I didn't tell her. I just told her that I needed to take a mental break. Which was true. I refused to tell my mentor, my guidance, my supporter, the reason that I was hopeful. I refused to tell her that I had to go to jail. I remember sitting in her office, when I first told her that I wasn't going to be returning next semester. I cried, and I told her, "I can't be here! I need a break. I need a mental break." She didn't question me. She said, "Okay. But when you need me, you call me!. You reach out to me! And you come back!" But you know what she did? She made me promise one thing to her. That I will be back.

I had to promise Dr. Calloway I will return and I will return quickly. I told her I will return in a year. We agreed that I would return back to school in a year. So here I am sitting in jail writing about returning back. But in the letter I wrote a confession, I told her I had been in jail. And that I am ready to come back and I need housing, I need scholarship, I need a job, and I have felonies. I need to know how to come back. I needed to know if she was still going to mentor me when I came back. It wasn't if I came back, it was when I came back. She wrote back quickly. And said, "Yes!"

I returned back to Eastern Michigan University. It was bittersweet. It was hard. Here I am on campus. I didn't have friends that I recognized anymore because some had graduated, some had moved on, some had dropped out of school. I had to reconnect myself to my environment. Just as I had requested, Dr. Calloway helped me find graduate housing. She helped me get a scholarship called the KCP Program that would pay for my books, it would pay for my tuition, it would also give me living expenses dollars. Along with that, she also helped me get a job as a graduate assistant. I worked for a teacher. Helping to teach class, helping to tutor students, helping to correct tests and quizzes.

Here I am a graduate assistant. I'm a felon. I'm a felon graduate assistant. I think that's when I began to experience what I call now, it's like a two-ness. And I get the two-ness from W.E.B. Debuois' book, "The Souls of Black Folk," where he talks about there's a two-ness for Black America. The two-ness of being black and being integrated. For me, my two-ness was being a felon-graduate student. There were things I still did that reminded me I was a felon. I slept in the dark with a light on just like in the prison cell. We had total darkness and the only light you saw was the bathrooms area. In order for me to go to sleep, my sleep settings had to be similar. My eating habits had to be similar. I had to eat morning, noon, and night. My regimen was to eat three times a day. I wasn't used to eating three times a day before. What I ate was different. I could no longer eat meat. I ate bread, potatoes, and other stuff. But, I did not eat meat. Absolutely no meat.

My father had to make me, a year or two later, eat chicken. Reason being I was beginning to become extremely anemic. And the doctor believed that it was because of my time in jail. But also too, because of my inability to consume meat products. And so my dad was firm with me and said, "You goin' eat that chicken!" So I ate chicken at least. But dietarily things changed for me. Uhm, my sleep patterns changed. How I interacted with people changed. I wouldn't dare tell anybody on campus that I was a felon. The only one that knew was Dr. Calloway. My secret was safe with her. Of course, she's a licensed therapist. Confidentiality, so I could confidently tell her how I felt. And then I would feel comfortable with disclosing certain things to her. But even with her the shame was still there. I didn't want to disclose to her what was going on.

For those who are getting' back in the world, I have three suggestions for you, maybe four, okay I will give you four:

1. **Before You Get Out, Have a Plan**

That's going to help you get out. Mentally I had to prepare to get out. I had to have a plan. That plan gives you a position for success. You have to position yourself for success. Planning brings position. You have to identify your position in anything you do. Even if you are already out. And you are reading this book and you say, "You know what, I'm out here. I have been out here for a year. I have been out here for three years. Let's start over." I want you from this point forward to plan something. I want you to plan your position. I don't want you to think that position is silly. In fact I don't want you to share that position with anyone. This position is a conversation between you and your position. It is very important that you conceal certain things when you are planning. Because you don't want outside influences to dictate the direction of your position. You have to become responsible for your position. I want you to identify your plan for success in that position. Because your position gives you a footing on what you're going to do next.

2. Plan Your Position

Okay, so the second thing you do after you plan your position. You identify some goals. I'll give you an example of a position and then I'll give you an example of a goal. So if your position is to buy a house because you want to have a place to stay for you, or for you and your kids or whatever. That's your position. You have to set a plan. So your goal can be to buy that house in two years. To buy that house in one year. You got your position and now you got your goal.

3. Create an Objective

The third thing you have to do is set, what we call in counseling therapy is to create an objective. Your objective tells you how to get there. So there are some things that need to be done before you get there, right? So your objective could be, you have to pull your credit. Okay. Your objective could be you got to find a job that supports being able to purchase a house. How are you going to do it? You are going to reach out to someone who can help you deal with your credit. Maybe like the credit man that I talk about. Reaching out to someone who helps you deal with your credit. See there are resources out here. You have to be mindful that for every problem there's an opportunity for a solution. Success is about creating solutions for yourself. Don't ever feel like you're stuck. Because the minute you're stuck, guess what? You're stuck. It's point blank. I have no philosophy any stronger than that. The minute you think you're stuck, you are stuck. And I want you to understand that you are never stuck. You have to look in the mirror, and you have to tell yourself: " I am brilliant! I am capable! I am blessed!" You have to speak affirmations to yourself: "I have the ability to succeed! I have the ability to be successful! Look yourself in the eye in the mirror and tell yourself you have to be successful. Why? Because that's what you were designed to be. That is part of the Success Lockdown. You have to lock down your success mentally.

4. Success Lockdown

Which brings us to my fourth point. Success Lockdown is about creating your success. We talked about your position, we talked about your goal, we talked about setting your objective. Now, Success Lockdown. You have to speak success to yourself. See, what you think, is what you do. I always say this, "poverty hits your mind, long before it hits your pockets." You have to create the success and the strategy is how you do it. So if you want to buy that house, you've gotten a job, you've secured employment, you've maybe started a business. You don't have to put yourself in a position where you say, "Oh, I can't find a job." Guess what? You create the job. You are capable. Start a business, find a business consultant. Find a way to start that business. Find a niche, find something that you can put together. A service or a product and put it in the marketplace. Everybody is always buying something. You have to figure out what it is that you can sell and what they can buy. There's a lot of resources you can google. If you are low on money you can go to the free library and check out books. You can go to the free Barnes & Noble and look at books. You can go to the free Books a Million and look at books. These are some of my favorite stores. You have to be responsible for your success. Which goes into number four again. Success Lockdown. Create the Success through what you think and what you are doing. These are the four things that you have to do to make it count when getting back out into that world.

Chapter 3:
Getting Down to Business

Like I mentioned before, I didn't always want to start a business. I was kind of forced to do it. I had everything pointing in that direction. Whether I agree with it or not. One of the first influences I have had in businesses is, or one of my first influences I had in wanting to start a business came from my interaction with Dr. Tina Parkman. Dr. Tina Parkman took on the task to mentor me. It's very important when you go through a season in your life that you get the proper counsel and mentorship. I was blessed to have that type of mentorship from Dr. Parkman after my incarceration period. I had things going on with me I didn't even know I had. I was ashamed. I was confused. I was broken. I had all the things pointing in a negative direction in my life: Two felonies, hard to find employment, no money. All I had was a position. I had a goal. I had an objective.

I had a reason to Lockdown my Success. I had to recover. I had embarrassed my parents and embarrassed my family. Hell, I embarrassed myself when I went to jail. I feel like I let everybody down. What I didn't realize at the time is, I was feeling that I let myself down. I was so concerned with who else I let down, I didn't really realize that the first person that I let down was myself. But I wasn't able to verbalize that at the time. When I had an opportunity to talk with Dr. Parkman, she was able to speak into my life that I needed a structure that would give me a basis for what I would be. That structure comes in the format of mentorship.

I can't urge you enough that if you have been incarcerated and you've come out, it's important that you find a mentor. A mentor may not necessarily be someone that's in front of you. Sometimes you can be mentored by people you have never met. I read a lot of books. I listen to a lot of people in the motivational speaking world. And as I listen to their teachings and I read their material I receive an impartation of them though I have never met them. They mentored me in many ways. And so, if you can't find someone physically to mentor you, I recommend that you go to the library, go to the bookstore and find a book that can speak to your destination of success. What I did was have an opportunity to interact with Dr. Parkman in a way that saved my life. I was still dealing with suicidal ideations. I was still dealing with depression. I was still dealing with a lot of frustration.

All the "No's" in my life. "No you can't work here." Even down to the position of "No you can't live here." I didn't realize that certain apartment places would not even allow you access to their apartment when they do the criminal background check. It doesn't matter that you have money to pay for the rent. You may not get in that apartment because you have a felony. That happened to me. I was in my PhD program at Wayne State University, and finally found the perfect apartment downtown Detroit. And ready to pay my deposit, ready to get in there, and they called me and told me that I could not go because of my felonies. I was devastated again! I prayed so hard.

Thank God that He Blesses me in a way and "Favor is never fair." I know you have heard people say. Well Favor was definitely in my life because I cried out to the Lord, just to be honest with you. And I said, God , if I'm supposed to move forward in the direction that You are calling me to move forward in, I gotta see some light at the end of the tunnel. Because here I am, I'm at Wayne State, I'm accepted, I have employment finally, but now I do not have a place to stay. By the end of the day, I got a call back from the management company. They reviewed my felonies, and management actually decided to overturn their decision and give me a chance. Of course, I had stipulations on being there. But I was there. So, people don't realize. It's things as small as not being able to get into an apartment because of your felonies that can mentally take you back. That could have put me back mentally. But guess what? I had a position. I had a plan. I had an objective. I had Success I needed to Lockdown.

Dr. Parkman, when I interacted with her, had an approach that allows you to be comfortable. Could be the fact that she's an excellent therapist. She's an excellent mentor. She's an excellent friend. And I definitely consider her one of my sisters in life. But as that little sister, I needed a big sister to speak into my life. To encourage me to pursue the God given talents that God had put in me. I needed that so badly. And I remember one day I was speaking with her. And I began to tell her about dreams.

God, He deals with me in dreams, you know. And I began to dream about children being lost and displaced and moving about and they couldn't find their parents. And some of them were crying, and some of them were soiled, and some of them were just scared and afraid. And the children in my dream, they were looking at me, to lead them, to show them, to give them some resources. And I remember just doing the best I could in the dream to feed them, and to change the diaper, and just to do what I needed to do in those dreams that I would have. And I shared those dreams with Dr. Tina. And, Uhm, she pretty much showed me that God deals with me in dreams and that I have a purpose that I need to pursue. And that purpose is directly tied into me doing something in a business format that's going to help those populations of children and families. So, Uhm, I agreed, what do I do from there?

I remember also speaking to my pastor. Apostle Robert Hill, the late Apostle Robert Hill. And I met with him and my pastor Barbara Hill and I shared with them the same dream that I had been having. And they quickly agreed that there was a specific calling on my life that allowed me to experience what I experienced so that I could be a caveat for change for others to break free. At the time that was tied into what I was thinking as it relates to an organization that can do just that for children. So with the help of Dr. Tina, she introduced me to an amazing lady, Wendy. Wendy created my first Nonprofit Organization.

Now, when I first met Wendy she was like no one I ever met. To this day my friends Camilyah Johnson - Buxton and Marcus Baggs joke among ourselves that Wendy didn't really exist, she was just an angel that appeared to give us directions. All three of us paid her to start our non-profit organizations. She was easy to talk to and a great listener of the vision God gave me for an organization. She listened intently and encouraged me just as a cheerleader at a game. This meeting with Wendy was such a challenge because I had all the dreams in the world, I promise I did! But I didn't have any of the money to line up with the dream. Of course we never have the money to line up with the dream right. But I had faith! You know.

You gotta have faith when you're embarking on something new. Just because you don't have the resources, doesn't mean you don't pursue it. The Bible says that "Now faith is the substance of all things hoped for, the evidence of things not seen." Hebrews 11:1. Just because I didn't have it didn't mean I couldn't achieve it. Just because I didn't see it, didn't mean it wasn't there. Wendy said, "I will do your Nonprofit Organization but it's going to cost you $1000. A $1000 dollars!!! Oh, My God, where was I going to come up with $1000??? Well, I had a choice, either I pay my rent or I pursue this dream. Rent -- Dream? Crazy as I am, I said, you know what? I have been to jail, I gained 300 pounds and lost it, I'm crazy enough just to believe this. So, I took my rent money and I paid Wendy. Best move of my life.

Now I had a business, my first Nonprofit Organization. What do I do now? What do I do with this business? Just because you got all the paperwork together, doesn't mean you have the process together. I did not know the first thing about business. I started it. I knew as a 501(C)(3) Organization I could become eligible for grants. Grants are access to money that does not have to be paid back. And so here I am, I didn't know how to write grants at the time, but I had a Nonprofit Organization. I had a Board of Directors. I had a group of friends who agreed to be my Board of Directors because they supported my vision. We had meetings. I pretended to be a CEO (Chief Executive Officer). I didn't know the first thing about being a CEO.

I had to pretend to be a CEO. I remember my mother always telling me, "Baby you gotta fake it till you make it in this world." I had to fake it till I made it. I made it.

I remember applying for my first grant. It was about $5000. I used that grant money to help feed homeless youth in downtown Detroit. My friends and I were already doing that. We would put our monies together and we would make sandwiches and snacks and we would go around to the homeless down on Cass Corridor area and downtown Detroit. And just pass out food to people and talk to them. Just show some love to them. I really found that I loved the activity. I really wanted to do more. So when I wrote the grant, He gave us $5000 so that we could do more. Shortly after that, I wrote another grant, and got access to another $5000. Here I am, new business, $10,000. I said, okay, "What do you do now?" It sounds to me like you need an accountant, because I don't want to be in a position where I'm not being accountable for this money. I already got felons. I'm not going to be a felon and go back to prison because I'm embezzling. So I need an accountant. So I found an accountant and I met with her, and she laughed at me. I love her, even to this day. Paris Hodges, CPA (Certified Public Accountant), the best accountant any new business owner could ask for. Her expertise is bar none, but her love for people is even more so superb. Paris sat down with me and she encouraged me that as a felon, I would not get another felony because of embezzlement. And definitely for not under $10,000 embezzling. So she spoke to my fears of not going back. It's important that you find people in your life that will speak to your fears. I don't care if it's in a prison. I don't care where it is. You have to find a person that will speak to your fears and confirm your success.

Don't just listen to the street community. Some call it the street committee. Side note, the street community or street committee are people who do not have any reference for the information that they provide for you. They have no background or reference for the advice they are giving you. In fact, typically those points of advice could be unsolicited. So when you have a group of people giving you unsolicited advice or information that does not have any reference points or facts attached to it, you might be talking to the street community or the street committee. So, I had to identify who the street committee was in my life. I had to separate too, I had to separate them being friends and family. I had to separate them from being positive role models. I had to separate, are you imparting in my life - are you taking from my life. I had to compartmentalize people in my life because that's how I helped deal with my trust issues as a new Entrepreneur. I had to put people in categories.

I had to learn how to keep a lot of secrets. And I'm not talking secrets about, "Oh I did this or shouldn't have done that." I'm talking about things that I believed God was sharing with me to do. I was very cautious about who I shared that information with because sometimes, you can give somebody your ideas for business and for whatever reason, they will hate on you. And that feedback and their response could shatter your dreams. They could move your position based on the fact that their expectation of you is not what they think you should be doing. So out of personal failures they project their feelings onto you. So, in this after incarceration period, even if it's not incarceration, when you are dealing with business development or starting a business, starting an idea, try to be careful enough not to keep sharing it with different people. I think it's good to share it if you have already compartmentalized the people in your life.

Encouragers, discouragers, you have to give them titles. Sometimes get you a pencil and paper if you have to write it down. Discouragers vs Encouragers and I don't care if you have five discouragers and one encourager put the information in front of the encourager. Leave those discouragers to themselves. I'm not saying don't talk to them. I'm not saying distance yourself 'cause sometimes the people in that category are your family. They're your friends, could be your husband or wife. It could even be your own children. But identify who the encouragers and discouragers are in your life and separate that. You have to have people that speak into your life good willful things because that's what's going to help take you to the next level. So, Dr. Parkman was there for me.

I had Paris, the CPA that was there for me. I had friends that were on my Board of Directors that were there for me. My family wasn't quite sold on this yet. They couldn't understand why I couldn't just go get a job. They know I had felonies, but they just couldn't understand why I didn't just work hard in the job I had. I did work hard in the job I had. It's just $22k a year, and it wasn't going to do much for me for the rest of my life.

I lived in downtown Detroit, I needed to have another plan that was going to allow me to access another level of success. And financial success was important to me back then. And it can be just as important to me now. I don't want you to identify success with money, but I do want you to be cognisant that when you have access to additional financial assets, you do put yourself into a position for longevity and future financial success. Making a distinction between the two, it is important for me to share with you, that when you are starting a business, you have to think about the social aspects of the business, but you also have to think about the financial aspects of the business. The Nonprofit is designed for charitable causes. My cause at that time was to empower children, no matter what their situation was to become better human beings.

The grant money was used to do that. I didn't do it out of my own pocket. I utilized grant money to do this. There was still finances coming in. A lot of times we want to run and do a Nonprofit and you wear yourself out doing free work. You always want to balance the two. I was working 9 to 5 and I was working 5 to 9. I was working weekends. I was working extra. And I was having fun. I was getting fulfillment. But the truth is, I needed more income. So, one of the ways to do that is that I knew I needed to learn how to write grants. So I took a class to learn how to write grants.

One of the things that you have to do when you're setting goals for yourself to start a business is, you have to be okay with sacrificing for what you need to do to be successful. Did I pay rent? Yes I did. I probably made other sacrifices in my personal finances to pay that rent. I didn't get evicted, but I also paid Wendy to do my business. I couldn't expect Wendy to do this for me for free because that interferes with Wendy's business. But what I do want to share with you is getting down to business has to do with sacrifice. I didn't need cable at that season of my life. Why would I pay for cable? I paid for the internet because I needed the internet to make money. I began to look at things that I didn't need so I could move forward to work towards the things that I do need. I needed the internet. I needed a house phone because that became my office phone.

Cell phones were just becoming popular during that time. In fact, I think they still had pagers back then. So what I'm saying is sacrifice has to be a part of the forefront if you are going to be successful in going into business. I would see people going on vacations. I would see people buying new cars. I would see people do a lot of things that they could afford to do. And I wanted that. I knew in order to get there. I needed to be successful. I needed to secure additional finances. I needed to be more fiscally responsible. I needed to make sure that my credit was in a positive position to be able to move forward. I had a goal, I wanted to buy a house. And I knew I needed to have a past prime credit score. Prime is 620 the credit man shared with me. Of course you can get credit for a new house at 620 but imagine the lower interest rate if we just dealt with your credit and got you to a 720.

Now you can save money in the long run. So I had to put my wants in the back of my needs. My wants were that I wanted my house. My need was that I needed to get my credit score better. I needed to make better financial decisions. So what I'm saying in closing for this chapter is, "You have to set your position by the way you play your cards." My cards were yes I have the felonies but no I can't let you knock me down like that. I gotta punch you back. So the best way I punched back was, I started the business; I created revenue for the business; I worked with people that supported my vision for the business; and I made sure I stayed mentored up when it came to keeping the business in a position that was going to allow me to have Success Lockdown.

Chapter 4:
Starting the Business

So you are ready to start the business right? You have a few ideals that have been manifesting in your head for a long time now. Some of you may be creative. Some may be more creative than others. Some people need to be in the position where they can surround themselves with other people that are creative or just as creative as they are. My recommendation for you is that starting a business has to come from a place in which you are ready to give your dedication to.

When I say give your dedication to, I mean you need to be willing to devote time, energy, space and even some inner things inside yourself that you didn't realize you had in you to start the business. Starting a business can be simple in many ways. I believe the complexity of starting a business has to do with what you're willing to put in the business to allow the business to start to grow, and to flourish, and to take off to that level of success. Now remember success has different levels. There are different levels of success that you have to look at when you're starting a business.

One level of success is to actually come up with an ideal for the business. It could be something simple like wanting to sell baked goods. It could be something as extreme or complex as creating an invention. No matter how simple or complex it is, the success is that you come up with it. That's one level of success. Another level of success is you actually did something with that idea. You went and spoke to someone, got some feedback. You went and researched the topic related to the business. You researched the trends related to the business. You researched the market. Research could have been, you're on your cell phone and you're googling different things about that business. Who's successful in that business? Who are your competitors in that business? Maybe it's a business no one has thought about before. Maybe you don't have a lot of research to go on in that business. But the fact that you actually put time and energy in that business to research shows that there's another level of success that you've achieved. Now, another level above that for starting a business is actually filing the actual business with the state. A lot of people don't realize that you can say you have a business all day but if you do not put the steps forward to actually incorporate the business. The business is just in your mind.

I'm going to talk a little bit about incorporations for those of you who may not be familiar with that and why that's important. A lot of times people may go to their county clerk in their city and they may file for a DBA which is called Doing Business As. The DBA is a good step but there's a better step that could be achieved. You can actually go to your state business filing website, in the State of Michigan, the State of Florida, the State of Georgia, the State of Texas you actually put a filing in place. Those are the filings that you see people do when they are filing for their LLC (Limited Liability Company), S-Corp (Subchapter Corporation), or their C-Corp (Alternative to S-Corp).

The difference between the DBA and the corporation filings at the state level is this. Essentially when you're filing as a DBA you're just Doing Business As a sole proprietor. That means it's just you and you are maybe selling baked goods and whatever you have your business idea to do. Now, one of the things I speak to people about on a daily basis is making sure that you file on the state level versus the city level DBA.

It's a matter of going big or going home. I like that, going big or going home. Let me explain that to you a little bit more. Going big to me means you don't half do things. It means you either do it or you don't do it. I've mentioned this all the time. One of my pet peeves is when I meet someone and they say they are doing something on the side. "Oh I do hair on the side. I cook food on the side." Whatever you do on the side, you have to be real, you have to be intentional about what you are doing on the side. When you are starting a business and you are putting your commitment towards being an entrepreneur that idea does not deserve to be put on the side. That is a God given talent. That idea needs to be in the arena of the big players. That's the difference between going big or going home.

So going big is to go to the state and file your corporation, LLC, C-Corp, S-Corp. If you don't know the tax implications then I say, google it or contact CPA (Certified Public Accountant), or someone in business who can give you some feedback on the differences. I will give you my feedback on it. An LLC is a Limited Liability Corporation. They have a lot of benefits to them because it allows you to be protected. Here's a distinction that you may want to know between the two different types. Okay, DBA vs. LLC. Let's just say you have the idea to create a business selling cupcakes. You are selling cupcakes at a local market or in your neighborhood. When you go to sell the cupcakes, you sell them to Johnny across the street. And Johnny happens to get sick from eating your cupcake. Well, Johnny gets sick from eating your cupcake and now Johnny has an interest in suing you because now Johnny says you caused him illness and had he not eaten your cupcakes, he wouldn't have gotten sick. Now you have opened yourself up to a lawsuit as a sole proprietor. Different scenario, you are a Limited Liability Corporation, LLC you have limited liability, okay. So you have these cupcakes and you are Cupcakes LLC and you sold some to Johnny across the street and Johnny got sick. Not that Johnny can't sue you, but that LLC protects you and gives you limited liability. So now the liability of the lawsuit falls on Cupcake LLC and not you, the owner. And so, you want that extra layer of protection for your business. Because as a business owner, you want to be able to make sure you are minimizing your risks as the CEO of that company. In that scenario it is very important that you understand that when you are starting a business you may have the better benefit of the business by forming an LLC vs DBA. Because in the DBA, you are personally liable for that lawsuit, in a LLC the LLC itself is liable for that lawsuit, okay. So with this description that I have just given you, this is the difference between going big or going home. So, actually starting a corporation helps you to begin to set up that standard of success. So now you're successful. Now you have the LLC. Now you can also file the LLC on the Schedule C of your personal taxes because now you are a business owner. So now that is an added benefit of being a business owner. You are able to get your proper tax write-offs in the business as an LLC.

The difference between a LLC, C - Corp, and S - Corp is the C - Corp and the S - Corp allow you to actually be a bigger player in the business world. In short the LLC and C - Corp have the same functions, there are different responsibilities between the two. LLC is very low maintenance in terms of operating a business. With the corporation, C - Corp or S - Corp , there are more details that you have to be cognisant of. In fact, you actually have shares that you can get access to investors, sell shares to your company, do a lot of nice things as it relates to building up this company. Depending on the company idea, I recommend LLC, vs C - Corp, vs S - Corp, so it varies on the different businesses. I want you to know that these three words exist so you can begin to build up your business terminology and vocabulary. Because as a business owner and entrepreneur you want to make sure that you are versed in knowing what you are getting yourself into as a CEO. So make sure you understand that a DBA is different from an LLC. An LLC is different from a C - Corp and a C - Corp is different from an S - Corp. Tax wise, the

C - Corp opens you up to double taxation S - Corp does not. I won't give you complexities right now because it's too early but I do encourage you to google, research, talk to tax professionals and CPAs and make sure that you're always researching and becoming more knowledgeable about your business and your business practices. I just walked you through different levels of success when you are going after starting that business. I want you to be cognizant that as you are starting the business you don't often find a place where you can get access to information readily. What I mean by that is, there are a lot of places and resources in different communities that you can go to. But sometimes, as a new business owner, you need some more concrete information. You need to have some assurity. You need to have some confidence builders. You need to have some things that are going to help you actualize what it is that you want to do in business that can actually be done.

To get that type of resource, I definitely recommend reading again. One of the most powerful tools you will ever have for building a successful business is reading. Reading is going to be your major requirement as a successful entrepreneur because now you are learning to adapt to the business world. You're going to begin to develop a two-ness, one as a felon, and two an entrepreneur. So that two-ness is always going to be there. However, you want to begin to strengthen your areas of information as it relates to business so that you can begin to have that balance. Just like you knew when they were going to have feeding time in lockdown, just like you knew when it was rec time, just like you knew when it was time for lockdown. You are going to learn those same different things for the business world. But you have to have that balance to bring them both together because it's a two-ness but the worlds will intertwine. That's not going to be overnight. It didn't take overnight once I started my business. It didn't take overnight to become the business person that I am today. That is twenty years plus in the making. I believe that you can do it. I believe that the fact that you are taking advantage of an opportunity to access this book, Success Lockdown. You've really taken some success steps the first day by picking up the book and actually getting this far in the book in this chapter. I commend you for that.

Nobody is going to be your greatest cheerleader other than you. I'm going to say that again because I need you to understand that no one is going to be a better cheerleader than you. You have to learn how to cheer yourself on, especially as a new business owner. Second, as a new business owner with felonies, you are going to have to learn how to applaud yourself when nobody else is applauding you. You are going to have to learn that self talk, that self encouragement. Doing things that are going to help you understand that you have to do this business. You have to pursue your dreams related to this business. There are going to be days when you are going to want to give up and I don't blame you because the business could be hard. It could be very difficult to sell a service or a product when you've never done it before. Especially when you have never had an opportunity to do that. You may be operating with no previous sales experience, no exposure.

But, I can tell you one thing, I can guarantee you one thing. You can not fail at something you have never done before. I tell myself all of the time when people approach me and I'm giving new ideas and options. I have this mindset that I can't mess it up because it ain't never been done before. There's nobody in front of me that has ever done this. There's nobody that I can use as an example to get things done. So, I tell myself often I can't mess this up. You're going to have to develop that self-talk, that self-evaluation, that you're okay, you can do it. And you can! One of the things that you have to look at, while you are trying to do it is, starting a business has its challenges. But the sweetness is the success of being able to make that first dollar while not working for someone else. I mean that first dollar that is made off of the sweat of your own brow, for your own company, you can't buy that anywhere. I remember the first time I started my business and the grant that we received. I worked hard to write that application.

And when that check came in for $5000, I was so happy. I mean I can't explain it. It was just like, WOW!, do you know how many hours I have to work making $22k a year to get access to $5000 right now? There's nothing like that first dollar that you make with your own business. And then to take that success that you've achieved with that first dollar that you made and say, "you know what?, if I could do it this time, I can do it again. I can do it again. You duplicate it, you build up your confidence in it.

I want you to know that building your confidence in business is no different than building your confidence as an athlete, as an actor, a performer, or an entertainer. Your first show will always be your weirdest, strangest show. But there is something about the fire in your heart, the fire in your mind, the fire in your mouth when you speak and you are getting things pushed out on a level that's going to allow you to actualize the success that you want to see. You have to put yourself in positions to lock down your success. Cheer yourself on, the fact that you came up with the idea, you reached a mark of success. You researched the idea, and you reached another mark of success. You filed your corporation, you reached another level of success. You put together a marketing idea or plan another level of success. You get my point? Everything you do relating to building that business after you started it, you are building your Success Lockdown mode. Building your Success Lockdown mode feels good and it should feel good because you put yourself in position to win.

You think while you are working 9 to 5 for someone else YOU are winning? No, THEY are winning. Do you know what they won? They won YOU. They won YOUR hard work. They won YOUR dedication. If you're late for work, you know what's going to happen, they know what's going to happen. I'm not telling you to be late for work because I want you to be on time for your job. I'm a firm believer in this, you will treat your job better than you treat YOUR own job. But you also have to have a level of good stewardship with other people. The Bible says we have to be accountable and I'm sure I'm paraphrasing, you have to be accountable for the things that you have. So, if I can trust you to be accountable for that 9 to 5, then I can trust you to be accountable for YOUR own 9 to 5. Building up your own business means you have to put together a work ethic. The same work ethic that you used when you showed up on time for that job, you have to put in that same level of work ethic for your own business.

There are so many things you have to consider when you're starting your business. You have to consider the resources that you have available for that business. You have to consider if this business is even fitting for this season in your life. I remember coming out, I always wanted to be a business owner that allowed myself to have the flexibility to come and go as I please. But I also wanted to have the flexibility of being as creative as I wanted to be in that business. So, having those things in place, I knew that I needed to be consistent with what I was doing in that business. Being consistent is very important as a new business owner. Making sure you are putting in your sweat equity. Sweat Equity? I got that term from the late George Johnson. A good friend of mine, Camilyah Johnson Buxton, Ed.S, Inkster, Michigan, introduced me to her dad. Great man, he was no stranger to hard work.

I remember sitting out in Inkster. He showed me a school that he had just gotten access to and he wanted to turn it into a tutoring center. We had to do different events and fundraisers to actually get that going. But what I remember most is the time that I spent with Mr. Johnson and him teaching me the importance of giving back to my community and serving my community. He also taught me the importance of Sweat Equity. Sweat Equity, I laugh when I say it. I can hear him say it like I did all those years ago. He said, "Young lady, Sweat Equity is when you work your but off for free! You are not going to get nothing out of it except the satisfaction of knowing you built some character, some ethics, some work commitments and some things that are going to help you be a better person. You didn't get paid monetarily. You got paid socially and psychologically. So the truth of the matter is, he told me, you are working for free today. But it will pay off for you years later."

I loved Mr. Johnson, and he was right. Mr. Johnson shared with me Sweat Equity, I wouldn't have known the importance of volunteering, giving back and being able to dedicate myself to something that would dedicate itself to me for the rest of my life and that's business ownership. So, Sweat Equity in the form of working for yourself and not necessarily getting paid right away. But knowing that you are building up something that is going to be lasting, something that can leave a legacy for your family and your kids, knowing that you can build it to something big and it's all yours. It's no different than Bill Gates. It's no different than Oprah Winfreys. It's no different than the Tyler Perrys. It's no different than the Jay Zs. Each one of those individuals had an idea. They put Sweat Equity into that idea and they built it into an empire. An empire that's going to lead them into a legacy that lasts for years and centuries long after they're gone. Somebody somewhere will still be talking about a Oprah Winfrey, a Tyler Perry, a Jay Z, a Bill Gates and last but not least, my favorite, a Martha Stewart.

With that being said, I wrap this chapter up by saying this, "You have the capacity to build anything that you put your mind to. Having a felony has its challenges. It has its setbacks. But I want you to close your eyes. I want you to think of a blank canvas. I want you to see that canvas as yours. Your canvas, you are in charge of that canvas. You pick the colors. You pick the pictures that go on it. You pick the type of theme you want that canvas to have. It's your canvas because it's blank. I want you to write on your canvas what you want to write. The type of business you want to have.

Get a vision board and write down what you want to do for your business. Don't ever let anybody tell you that dreaming is silly. You will never get anywhere if you don't dare to dream. I know you've heard this a hundred times but I'm going to tell you a hundred and one times. Do not be afraid to dream. Do not be afraid to paint on your canvas. And whatever you decide to put on that canvas. I want you to be proud of it. If it's a stick figure, it's YOUR stick figure. If it's a beautiful mural, that's YOUR beautiful mural. If it's just lines and beautiful colors, those are YOUR lines and beautiful colors. That's YOUR business, that is YOUR business idea, that is the baby that YOU are choosing to raise. Think about YOUR dream. Set a plan for YOUR dream. Go after YOUR dream. Go ahead and Lockdown your Success. It's all YOURS!"

Chapter 5:
Credit to Your Race

When you get your business started, one of the things that is the most asked question is what do we do about funding. Everybody wants to know about business funding as it relates to starting your business. You need the funding. You need the capital to be able to exist. You need to be able to buy the things you need to start that business, to grow that business, to market that business. All those things take money, right? A lot of times there's no plan in place for business owners who are looking to start a business. The reason being is they don't know about the resources or the opportunities to access these resources through credit.

Credit is so important for anyone, especially the felon. Because, I know, one of the things that happened to me while I was incarcerated was my credit was compromised. Someone got access to my credit profile. They started buying things and they got access to credit cards. I had Discover cards. Growing up in my family, my family always paid for things with cash. We were a cash purchasing family. I never knew the importance of credit. I didn't know about interest rates. How credit affects the interest rate. I didn't realize that when someone extends credit to you, it's based on the credit reporting system from three bureaus, TransUnion, Equifax, and Experian. Of course, my credit man would tell me that there's other credit reports that I need to be aware of as well. But let's just stick to those three. Those three tell your story. They decide if you are going to get housing. They decide if you are going to get that new car. They are going to even decide if you are able to open up a checking account or open up an insurance policy. They even decide if you can get cable in your house. Sad, but it's true, credit does run the world. Credit can ruin your world. So having a good credit score is good and it's important for you to be cognisant of. Not just for the interest rate, but also for the fact that you are building your new business. As I mentioned, my credit was compromised while I was locked down and many people are. Because they know, that's the best way to get access to someone's credit because they are going to be gone for a period of time. They bank on you not checking on your credit. So, while I was there incarcerated, those credit cards were applied for and used. They were charged up and then debt collectors came after me. I didn't even know what bills that they were talking about because I had no knowledge of credit and what it was for and what it was not used for. So, a lot of times we look at credit as something to be ashamed of because as a felon, that was just one more thing to be ashamed of. Not only am I a felon, not only can I not find a job, not only may I be denied housing, but now I have to deal with having bad credit. And I don't know how to get my credit in a better position because I don't understand the laws or the rules regarding the Credit Report Act. So, what do you do? You have to always seek the knowledge of others and take on the information that others are giving you. Business is about connecting with the right people that can bring you the right resources to take you where you need to go in business. As it relates to my credit, I was introduced to a gentleman who showed me how to pull my own credit report. I was afraid to pull that credit report the first time because I didn't want another strike against me. My credit was not good at all. He showed me line by line what happened. He also showed me the fraud that had occurred on my credit report too. While I was looking at that, I wanted to buy a house. I had a goal, right? But, I couldn't buy a house with my credit report looking like that, you know? He said I could become eligible because I was at least prime, 620. But, I wouldn't get a good interest rate. Interest rate meaning I wouldn't be allowed to have an affordable monthly payment. Had I just gotten my credit up 100 points, 720, then that would lower my payments. It doesn't change the amount of house but it does change the amount I am paying monthly for the house. He said, just give me a year. Let's get your credit in a better position so that we can get you access to a house. Now, what he did was amazing. He actually challenged the credit bureaus about the errors on my credit report. After sending letters to different people, creditors and people who said that I owed them, he was able to get those derogatory marks removed from my credit.

    In addition to that he taught me the word Secured Credit Card.

Secured Credit Card, what is that? A Secured Credit Card is a credit card that you can go to your bank or financial institution, you can put X amount of dollars on it and it will show up on your credit report as if it is a credit card. When you use it, you are using your own money. You use it and you pay it, and that builds up your credit. So while he was removing derogatory information off my credit, he was also having me add positive things on my credit. Then, after that, I was able to apply for department store credit cards and that would repeat that, I would do the same thing. I would charge something and I would pay it off. I would charge it, I would pay it off. Little by little, my credit score increased over 700.

I'm saying all of this to you for a reason. I want you to understand that as a business owner, you need to have yourself in position for a positive credit rating. If you have a credit score of 700 and above, you have access to capital, business credit, okay. I work with a very strategic partnership of individuals that credit is their wheelhouse of knowledge. What they do is, they work with non-traditional business owners. A non-traditional business owner is a person who may not have had any background experience in starting a business. They could even be in a business that is not traditional. A non-traditional business could be a business that is out of your home, a business that does not have a storefront. A business that is run on your mobile phone, off of your tablet, it's non-traditional in a lot of ways. I consider myself a non-traditional business owner because I didn't have formal training in business. I have lots of years of experience in business development. That's where my non-traditional business expertise comes in because where you are at, I have been there. Where you are going, I have been there. I wanted to always be a resource for people like you to have the information you need so that you can get to where you need to be in business without having to experience the bumps and the bruises and the scrapes that I have experienced in business.

Getting the business started is a great step. The essential next step is, (and you do this at the same time while you are getting your business started) you have to address your personal credit issues. I know it could be an ugly credit report. It can make you look like the worst person in the world. But you know what? When you are able to work with a professional team or a person that can deal with those credit issues. It's like on TV when you see people get a makeover. This would be like a credit makeover for you. Credit professionals are going to teach a lot. They will teach you that everything creditwise is just fictitious documentation that needs to be addressed properly to make sure the errors on your report do not affect your credit history. Your credit is like your financial resume and you need a professional to make sure that your credit resume allows you to become successful with that document. I'm not quite sure my credit man would have said it just like that but this is just my opinion of what is said and what it does for you in your business. And then think about what it does for you psychologically. You know what? When my credit score went from 620 to 720, you couldn't tell me nothing! I'm just going to tell you, I felt like a credit rock star. I had an opportunity to get a new car with a great interest rate. There's a difference between having "A" credit for getting a car and having "D" credit rating when you apply for a car. I didn't understand early on how good a credit score needs to be to be effective for where you are going. I'm telling you 700 and above push you in a good position as a business owner. Because you are now able to have access to funding sources that will fund your new business.

Now you will get people who will tell you, "Don't use credit for your own business." They have their reasons why, they think that's a great idea. I have my reasons why I think it's logical to be able to access business credit. There are many businesses that I have started by accessing business credit. Had I not accessed business credit, I wouldn't have never been able to start that business. I would have been somewhere trying to figure out how to get somebody to invest in me without me investing my own dollars. You see how that sounds, right? If someone approaches you, and they say, "hey, I want you to invest $10 in my business, but I don't want to invest my own $10, I want to use your $10." You are going to be looking at them like, really? That's exactly how some investors look at you. You have to be willing to put your own dollars on the line sometimes. Now, there's a lot of Shark Tank examples and a lot of different scenarios that people are able to secure investors in. That's great! I want you to know that those deals are one in a million. If I were you, I wouldn't put my eggs all in one basket! I'm telling you, being practical and savvy is one of those characteristics that you are going to have to have in order to be successful as a business owner. Remember, we are not talking about just any business owner, we are talking about a business owner with felonies. We have to be savvy. We have to be strong. We have to be knowledgeable. We have to be courageous. We have to put ourselves in positions to be successful.

One of the ways in which I put myself in a position to be successful is I leveraged my credit to access some funding to start a few businesses that have been very successful for me. I say all of that to you to say this, "That credit score will help increase your chances of getting access to the resources." Now you also have to have this going on for yourself too as well. Are you accountable for the amount of money that you are going to receive? I mean for businesses that we have started and that I have partnered with, we have had to put in $40k - $60k a piece to start those businesses. Now you are thinking about two or three things when you have to do something like that:

1. Can I trust my partners to put my $50k or $60k in the basket with theirs ?
2. Do we have accountability in place to account for $50k - $60k x3 ($150k -$180K)?
3. Is my partnership strong enough to sustain that type of investment from myself into that business too? Is there accountability? Do we have an accountant? Do we have checks and balances? Do we all have access to accountants? Are we just pulling money out or are we setting up a system?

We have to be practical. Don't ever put your money into anything without having a solid plan. And do not ever develop a solid plan for any business without any documentation. You need a legal binding contract between you and those business partners. You also need a binding contract on who is responsible for what in that business. So when you look at partnerships, you have to look at partnerships like it's a marriage.

The same thing when you are partnering with your cash because you have accessed business capital for your business. You have a partnership with that lender, you agreed to pay that lender back. That lender is depending on you to meet the terms that you agreed to receive that loan or that credit extension to you. So making sure that you have the moral standard to be an entrepreneur is very important. Don't you touch money and dare to think it's okay not to pay it back. Now things do happen, business ideas start; you have intentions on paying it back; business fails. I'm not saying that doesn't happen because it does happen, it will happen, I have failed a lot in different businesses. One because I'm not afraid to jump into a new business. If it feels good, I will jump into it. I have to do research on it. I have to do my due diligence. I do a lot of checks and balances on it. But I'm not afraid to dream. I'm not afraid to fail either.

Failing gives me an opportunity to succeed at another time. I don't want you to feel like, "Oh, I don't want to start this business. I don't want to get access to this cash or credit because what if it fails? You have to ask yourself, what if it doesn't?" Just like I have had a lot of failures, I have had a lot of successes in business. Those failures have balanced me. Those successes have balanced me. You have to have that balance. The things that I failed at in business, for whatever reason, it taught me, it grew me. The gray hairs on my head gave me wisdom for the next things I would do in business.

When you get into a business partnership and you think that this partner is going to be there with you and help carry the burden, the weight and the load, and you guys are working, then something happens. That partner is not the partner you thought he or she was. Now the business is failing. I have been there and done that. But, I didn't stay there. Knowing when it's time to jump out of a partnership is wisdom. Knowing when you have been taken advantage of, that's wisdom. Some people don't dream because they are scared that they are going to be taken advantage of. Guess what? You are being taken advantage of already, because you have heard this before. If you are not building YOUR dreams, YOU are building SOMEONE ELSE'S dreams.

Every time you report to somebody else's place of business to make them millions of dollars and you are not thinking of a way to make yourself millions of dollars, guess what? You are taking advantage of yourself. You are letting them take advantage of you. I'm saying all of this to say to you, "I want you to be a forward thinker when it comes to business. I want you to be a forward thinker when it comes to how you run a business. I want you to be a forward thinker when it comes to the importance of credit and accessing it to be able to gain access to cash so you can have access to resources so that you can start your business and grow your business.

Get you a good team. Put that team together. The team is just a counsel of experts in the area. I tend to put myself around sharper tools in my shed. I want sharper tools in my shed. I like when people are smarter than me. I say this all of the time. The smartest thing I ever do in business is I put people smarter than me around me. I want them to be experts opposite of me because that creates the team. That creates the position that I can become more successful and I can lock down my success more successfully because I have a team in place.

I love being able to go back to my team and ask them, "Should we do this? Should we do that?" A lot of times, people get offended when they have to ask people something. Do not ever run that perception in your mind that you have to be smart to be a business owner. Yes, you have to be savvy, you have to have some intelligence, you have to be knowledgeable now. But do you have to know everything? No you don't! The secret is you have to be able to assess everything. You have to have access to people that know everything. I'm okay with not knowing everything in business but because I surround myself with like-minded business focused individuals. I also surround myself with people who are experts in their area. My credit man, you cannot beat him in knowledge related to credit. When I have a question about my credit. I go to him because I know he's going to have an answer. In fact, I have a diverse group of credit professionals that I work with. I work with three or four different ones because I have a track record with them number one. Number two, I appreciate all of their different approaches dealing with derogatory information on credit reports. I appreciate their giftings, and their knowledge base. I recommend that these individuals are in positions to help people like you when it comes to building your credit up and getting your credit in a position so you can access business credit.

Credit to your Race, you know what the race is? The race has nothing to do with your skin tone. The Race is the Race to the top. The top of what? The top of our game, the top of your achievements, the top of your success. I'm telling you, if you're going to lockdown success, you are going to have to get serious. You are going to have to go places that nobody else is going to go with you at. You're going to have to be willing to go to places that no one is going to want you to go. Want to know why? Because it's not their comfort level. Sometimes people get comfortable with you being mediocre.

You are never going to be able to be ordinary anymore in your mind. You're going to move from ordinary to extraordinary. Okay. Because the minute you find that you are taking yourself out of the equation of ordinary, guess what? You have just stepped into the land of extraordinary. Once you hit that land of extraordinary, you are on your way to locking down success in a way that only you can actualize. Your mother can't actualize it, your father can't actualize it, your brother, sister, friend, cousin. No, you have to actualize it.

I am a first generation college student. I am a first generation business owner. When my parents kept asking me, "Why can't you just keep a 9 to 5 or go to a 9 to 5 or just work 9 to 5?", I didn't want to keep that 9 to 5 because I had other plans on my mind. I knew I had more things in me. In order to get those things out of me. I had to step out into an arena. See, remember with felonies, we can't go everywhere that everybody else can go. See, people take that for granted. People think, "Oh, you can just get a job here or you can get a job there." No, we don't have those types of luxuries. I have a PhD and I can't imagine being able to get to the levels that I deserve to be without having business ownership in my pocket. Not only have I employed myself, but I have also been able to employ others and to teach others just like you the importance of entrepreneurship and growing and building a successful business off of their service or their product.

So for locking down your success, one of the keys to that is having a successful credit score. Grab hold to that key. Pull that credit score. Find out what that credit score is. Resolve your credit score issues. Find the resources you need to deal with that credit. Get access to some business funding. Set your marketing plan with that funding. Don't ball out of control with that funding. You have to set a standard of being accountable. Remember, accountability in business ownership is very, very important. You have to be able to be trusted and be trustworthy in business. Take that money and make it matter. Don't go buy a new car, don't go buying stuff for your business that you don't need to have. Don't go spending X-amount of dollars on a website. Don't do this, don't do that.

Do you know what one of my practices is when I get access to business funding? When I create a budget for what it is that I want to purchase and things that I need to purchase to get that business off the ground. I quickly say no to each of those items and I create justifications on paper to turn those no's into yeses for purchases for my new companies. It works. It helps to create accountability and it also helps me to evaluate. Remember self-evaluation is very important in business. It helps me to self-evaluate my spending for my business.

Listen, I want you to be successful in this business. I am going to keep giving you real information that is going to help you lockdown that success.

Chapter 6:
Business Operations

You've gotten to the point where you've started the business. You have done the proper filing, whether it be a LLC, C - Corp or S - Corp. You have taken the appropriate steps to start your business. Now it's time to get organized. This happens at the same time that you start the business because getting organized is a very important step in business development. Now, let's talk a little bit about business development and that word because it can be a little frightening hearing those words together at the same time.

Business Development is essentially, the creation of a company and the developmental steps it takes to grow that company and allow that company to experience all of the processes and systems that need to be created in order for that business to operate effectively. Now, anyone can have a business, it's just a matter of filing the proper paperwork. What you do want to consider is the fact that when you start a business, you want a business to have a strategy for that business to be successful. Part of your strategy should include ensuring that your business operations are in proper order.

The development of a company, especially new companies, needs to be in a place where you can identify the goals for starting that company's success. Here we go again with the word goals. Anytime you do anything related to business you have to consider that goals are going to be at the forefront of making sure anything that you do becomes effective. Affectability transfers into success. With your business operations, you want to make sure that everything is in place. So one of the things that should be in place for business is accounting. Now a lot of times, people will say, "Well I can't afford a CPA" or are just starting out and that's fine.

You're right, it may be important that you build that business up and grow the revenues of that company so that you can put yourself in a position where you can afford that CPA. But there are so many tools out there available for you that you can use. There's a lot of software, you can actually google. When I first started my business, I used Quickbooks. Right now, Quickbooks has online capability, just like other products. So, with the products that you choose, that software is going to allow you to keep up with the different daily spending as it relates to your business. You have to have a budget because that budget is going to help become your guidance for operating that business.

Let me give you a quick example of a cupcake business, Cupcake, LLC. Everyone knows that in order to have a successful business, you have to have products to sell or services to sell. In this case, you are selling a product. You are selling cupcakes. So, there are ingredients in that cupcake that cost money. So you want to consider the flour and the eggs. You want to consider the special added things that you put in cupcakes. All of those items, you should list them down on paper and how much they cost. Then, what you do is once you list those things out and find out how much they cost. Go ahead and identify what you need to prepare those cupcakes. You need mixing bowls. You might not need anything. You might have everything you need right in your house and that's okay. You still need to list it out because you need to be accountable for the equipment that you use for that particular business. The whisk, the pan, the pot, whatever you need to make cupcakes. You have to list those things out. Now, you should always know how much it costs to produce that cupcake. Creating that budget helps you to identify that. Now that you know how much it costs to create that cupcake, you can begin to identify how much you are going to sell the cupcake for. You discover that when everything is broken down it costs you about $.50 to make each cupcake. You have a specialty cupcake, you have to research the market. There's a cupcake place that I love to frequently purchase from. Especially during birthdays, holidays and special occasions because these are the best cupcakes ever to me. They cost about $3.50 and sometimes depending on the cupcakes complexity, some of the cupcakes can be $4.00. But those are specialty cupcakes. Now what you want to do is, research your market. You want to research what's the going rate for specialty cupcakes. Once you have researched that, you want to also research the cost of other cupcakes in a regular retail store such as Walmart or Target. You want to begin to strategically price your cupcakes to be competitive to something that someone can just go to the store and pick up. You may be competitive with that but what you can't be competitive with is compromising on what you need to do to make that cupcake sell. You cannot compromise on that.

    Sales are very important. If you do not have sales as an experience. It may be important to bring on a partner to help you with sales. Or, get some sales consultant to help grow those sales of that cupcake. Remember, it's one thing to have the product, it's another thing to be able to sell the product. So, now you have the cupcake, you know the price point for the cupcake and how much to sell the cupcake for. Your input from your salesperson is important for helping you to determine that price. If that cupcake costs you $.50 to make you may say that you can sell your cupcake for $1.00. You just made 100% profit on that cupcake. Now with that profit you begin to create a budget of how many cupcakes you are going to sell each month. You may decide that you are going to sell 100 cupcakes a month. Let's do the math on 100 cupcakes a month. When you look at the math on that. 100 cupcakes at $.50 a cupcake, is $50. It's going to cost you $50 a month to make 100 cupcakes. But you are going to sell the cupcakes for $1.00 which allows you to have a $50 profit for the month.

    You look at that and say to yourself, "Hmf, that was a lot of work, the $50 is a pretty good profit, maybe I should sell those cupcakes for $2.00 a piece. So now you have put yourself into a stronger profit margin for selling those cupcakes. If you look at it like this, you are making those cupcakes $.50 and making $50. Now when you look at the profit margin on what you are doing by increasing the sales price to $2.00, you are selling 100 cupcakes for $2.00 and making $150 profit. That creates a profit margin of $150. The cupcakes are being made for $50 and sold for $200 creating a $150 profit margin. Now you have created an example budget of expenses versus profits in your business. So that's just one example that you can use for operating your business because budgets are very, very important.

Now, the other thing that you want to keep in mind is, making sure that you have agreements in place. I mentioned to you earlier that you want to bring in a salesperson to help you sell the cupcakes. That salesperson could be your friend, could be your family, could be anyone who's very excited about your business. But you always want to make sure that there's an agreement in place between you and anybody that relates to your business. One of the most horrible experiences that I've known has to always begin with the fact that people did not have agreements or contracts in place with people that they partnered with prior to the partnership. Sometimes you think that it's going to be an easy ride. But sometimes what you don't understand as a business owner, that people's intent may not be what it started out with originally. As months go by and profits go by, people's minds change and they think they should be compensated for more than what you have agreed to verbally.

To make sure that none of that or any of that becomes an issue for you in your new business, what you want to do is make sure that you put an agreement or contract in place. It may be very important for you to reach out to a business consultant or even an attorney or someone in the legal field that is able to help you create a contract or agreement to be able to bring on someone to work with you in partnership or work for you.

In the event that you are bringing on someone to work for you there's other decisions you need to make. You need to identify if that person is going to be an independent contractor or are they going to be an employee with a W-2. Here's the difference. When you work at a job 9 to 5 typically that job is a W-2 and you are an employee. Employees earn wages in which taxes are taken out of their paychecks at both the Federal and State level by that business or employer. You pay taxes or receive a tax refund at the end of the year when you file your income tax return as an employee. Now, as an independent contractor it's the opposite. That person is an independent contractor. They don't have set hours like 9 to 5. They come and go as they please regarding the operations of your business. For independent contractors, there needs to be a contract in place for them as it pertains to the services they are providing to your business. As an independent contractor they receive a 1099. Taxes are not taken out of their check at the Federal nor at the State level. They are responsible as independent contractors to pay their taxes directly to the Federal Government and at the State level. W-2 Employees and 1099 independent contractors are two very different things. You will have to make that decision when bringing someone on to work in your company and what will be best for your business.

When a new business is starting out I always recommend starting out with 1099. It gives you a couple of benefits. One, it allows you to test that relationship out with that person. It may be important for you to know early on if that person is going to be a long term person that you are going to work with. As you get to know that person, you are going to know if it's going to become a long term relationship working with them. Now, when it comes to a W-2 employee, that person has different rights as an employee. Hiring a person as an employee will require that you create an employee handbook. The employee handbook for best practices is something that creates a guide for employers to give to their employees as it relates to making sure that the company's rules are being followed and making sure that there are proper things in place. Now in order to have an effective employee handbook, I recommend that you reach out to a consultant who has the experience in putting together employee handbooks.

You will have to consider payroll when it comes to W-2 employees. As an employer with employees you have to be conscious of the fact that now you are responsible for payroll and payroll taxes. There are a lot of different responsibilities that a small company has to handle no matter how many employees are on payroll, whether it is just you and you are treating yourself as an employee or family member who's now your employee. Anytime there's an exchange of dollars from one person to another there's an importance that you have that handbook in place which is an agreement essentially for your employment opportunity to that employee. But you also have to make sure that this company also has a set of rules that work for everyone that works in that company. You can't have a special set of rules for your mother if she works for the company or another set of rules for your son that works for the company. You want to make sure that you keep those rules standard for everybody. That avoids lawsuits and things like that.

There's a term in business called risk mitigation. Risk Mitigation is, essentially making sure there are not any things in your company that could create a risk to create liabilities in your company. Let's talk a little bit about company risks and examples of company risks. Company risk for example, let's use the company of Cupcakes LLC. You have an employee and the employee is responsible for delivering the cupcakes to the consumer or the person who wants to purchase the cupcakes. Now that person becomes a delivery person. That person is using their own vehicle to deliver those cupcakes. That person gets into an accident. Now, who's at fault? That person is your employee so now they were in an accident under your company so you're in a position as a company owner to be sued because now you have the liability of making sure that the employee is taken care of as a person that worked in your business.

Now had the employee handbook had certain things in place you could have mitigated your risk for being sued in that company. For example, say that there's a contract that the person who drives their own vehicle uses their vehicle at their own risk. You have to make sure that the person is insured and you may say as a requirement for their job they have to use their own vehicle and they are responsible for turning in their registration and proof of insurance every so often in that company because they will be using their own vehicle for this job, not a company vehicle.

There are special business insurances that come in place when you have employees that will be driving their own vehicle as it relates to your company. Now, I know this is a lot of information but it's important for you to know because I need you to know that as a new business owner there are a lot of things that need to be considered especially when you have an employee in place. Another thing that you have to consider as it relates to risk mitigation is the fact that there are liabilities. Not only are there liabilities in the financial accountability of the company but you have to look at the liabilities of individuals that work for you.

A liability could be a person with a not so good driving record delivering in your company. Now it would be wise as a new business owner with new employees to do a background check. Now, here's that word again, because as a felon, we get upset because we can take our own personal experience and transfer that to our business. You have to think of yourself as a business owner now and not that felon. You may want to cut that person some slack because you are giving them a second chance but you have to look at now as a business owner the liability that the person can cause in your company if that person is not properly reviewed for a background check and it can affect your company. I'm not saying not to hire felons. I'm saying that you have to consider the risks as it relates to operating your new business.

You have to consider what you need to be effective and what you need to be able to grow a company effectively considering the circumstances that a person who has a not so good background may be a risk to your company. Now, there are other things you can do to mitigate that risk. There are different insurances that you can get that actually put a bond on felons that allow a felon to security knowing that because this bond is in place in the event something goes wrong in your company, that you do not assume all of the liability as it relates to that person working for your company. Those security bonds can be accessed through many insurance companies and when we talk about business insurances we will go over that a little bit more.

But just getting back to the fact that there are a lot of things that need to be considered when you are mitigating the risk in your new company. A background check review will help give you insight on whether or not that person is the best fit to drive for your company. Maybe that person's best fit would be to be in a sales position that does not allow them to drive or deliver. Now when we are talking about making sure mitigation of risks are implanted into your company, you want to make sure that you are looking at everything that has the potential to give you a liability. A liability is essentially a debt. One accident could really put your company at a disadvantage and also allow our company to close down. Also making sure that you have proper insurances in place helps to mitigate the risk in operations of your new company. There are a lot of things to consider but I want you to know these things. An accountability system, liability, risk mitigation, these are all terms I want you to begin to familiarize yourself with as a new business owner because these are the things that help you operate effectively.

We have talked about getting assistance from a business consultant; getting assistance from a legal person; getting assistance from someone that has the ability to do bookkeeping or accounting is very important. Insurance is also very important for your business. Insurance in business is essentially no different than you having insurance on your cell phone. That cell phone insurance is very important for you. In the event that you lose your cell phone or damage your cell phone, guess what? That insurance will allow you to get a new phone from that mobile phone provider. So these are all of the things that you want to make sure that you put in your business budget. The cost for that insurance that you get each month. The cost to be able to take that gas and deliver those cupcakes to the consumer. All of these things are pieces that you have to consider to operate the business.

It's a lot of information, but guess what? You can do it because you are reading this book; you are learning the resources; you are learning the things you need to learn to be able to have an edge on others who are starting their business. One, they don't know this information; two, they don't want to follow this information; and three, they just don't have anyone to coach them through this process efficiently to make sure that they have success. See, I want to make sure that you are able to lockdown success in your business. It's one thing to start a business, but it's another thing to start a star. It's one thing to start a business that's going to allow you to create revenue that will keep your business afloat for years and years and years.

With that being said, I want you to stay encouraged and know that the keys to locking your success in the business world have to do with your attitude and your ability to reach the heights and information. Reading is going to be the number one essential thing that you will need to do. Learning is an everyday thing, it's not overnight, this information will not just soak in overnight. But, over a period of time as you operate, as you grow, as you seek out counsel, you will be able to lock down the success that you need to have a positive and strong growing business. I'm going to focus on business operations for you for the next chapter. But in the next chapter I'm going to be a little more specific on what it is I need you to do to lockdown that success in your business operations.

Chapter 7:
Business Operations (Part 2)

Business Operations is an essential part of growing your business. I don't want any new business owner to get the expectation that the business world is super easy because it's not. It requires a lot of dedication and commitment. Sometimes it engulfs your whole life in the beginning. That means you have to make the sacrifices you need. I know that you can do it because. You've already spent a lot of time sitting and sacrificing. I was thinking about those times when I sat down in jail and just wasted time in my mind. But I didn't want to have a mindset that I was wasting time. So, I would begin to scratch down different ideas of what I would do if I was a business owner. In fact, there's a lot of business operations that go on just in the jails.

When we look at over the years that the prison system has privatized and they have put everything in a place where you see the money that's going back and forth. I was so shocked when I got out of jail a few weeks later and I received a bill from the jail for doing my jail time. I was shocked as hell. I have to admit I could not believe it, not only did I do time, not only did my credit report get compromised while I was in jail but dammit I got a bill for being in jail. That was one of those things that made me think that business is everywhere. That the incarceration system is nothing but a great big business. How did I know? Because I was one of the people who were sitting there just like some of you who are reading this book. While I was there something else surprised me about business. The commissary that we wore had Bob Barker's name on them. And you couldn't get me to understand for the life of me, you mean Bob Barker on The Price is Right? This guy? He has his own commissary? All of our commissary came from his company. Well, THE PRICE IS RIGHT, because those who have been in jail or even had to put money on someone's books because they needed to buy something in jail, know the cost of being incarcerated.

Whether it was buying snacks, buying clothes, even down to the point that when you call someone, that phone call is super expensive, it's too expensive. I probably spent more money in jail than the average person because I had a support system of people who would take that call from me. But for those who don't have that support system, for those who don't take that call from them, it could be very detrimental. I remember going to the phone and calling my parents and talking with them but then I would look back behind me and I would see so many other people who weren't able to call anybody. That was a sad time. For those who know what I am talking about and experienced the business part of the jail, you know that everything that they do has a business implication to it.

So, as I sat there in that jail. I could not get different business stuff out of my head because not only was the business in my mind for myself but there were other business ideas in mind of the others that sat in the jail cells with me. One thing you have to get rid of is the misconception that people that are in jail or prison are not bright. Some of the most brightest, strategic individuals are locked behind bars. The only difference between you and them is maybe you didn't get caught but they did. That doesn't make them stupid it just creates the position that everyone at any given time in their life can find themselves in a position of misfortune.

You try to make good choices throughout your life. You try to do the best you can throughout your life. Sometimes things get to you and you make bad decisions that can interrupt the rest of your life. But for those who have not allowed their circumstances of imprisonment or incarceration to represent the rest of their life, I want to tell you that I am proud of you. I am proud of you because you have made the effort and you have put the steps in place to lock down your success and grow beyond where you need to grow.

As we go through these chapters and I am sharing my experiences, I am also sharing with you the wisdom that I was able to access just sitting behind those jail cells. I was able to be creative. I was locked away from cell phones and all of the distractions of the outside world as we called it while we were sitting in there. But it also allowed me to be creative. It allowed me to develop a reading ethic. I read a lot of books while I was there. I prayed a lot while I was there.

I watched a lot of TV. That's why to this day, I refuse to watch TV because I spent a year watching television. I watched it then because it was a way for me to feel connected to the outside world, to the outside music, to the outside world of what's going on. The news was very rarely watched there. Some nights were news nights and we were able to see what was going on locally. Nationally, not so much. I think that the television situation really was guarded by the particular guard that was on security that night. So if that person felt like watching the local news, guess what? We had to watch the local news. No one particularly watched the national news, so we didn't watch the national news. But, television to this day, is one of the biggest distractions I see going on in society. In order to be effective in operating your businesses, you have to begin to develop self-evaluation, self-talk and you have to make great choices. A great choice for me is to read more than I watch television. For me, reading balances my mind and it gives me creativity. Watching television drains my creativity. Watching the news sometimes depresses me. I do find myself watching documentaries because of the content that is feeding my intellect. You have to feed your intellect. Your intellect is what guides you. Your intellect is what brings about your ability to be creative in your business.

Creativity is one of the number one requirements for being an effective business owner. Now remember, I told you, I don't want you to just be an ordinary business owner. I want you to be an extraordinary business owner. So, in order to have effective operations you need to be creative which leads me to the part two reason that I needed to carry over from the part one of business operations.

When it comes to business operations, you have to make sure that marketing exists in your company. Marketing is what guides you to growing your revenues in your company. Creating a marketing strategy could be as complex or as simple as you need it to be. Let's go over a little simple strategy that can be used. This is an exercise that I want you to use to challenge yourself when you're thinking about marketing. I am going to use the example of the cupcake business that we have been using throughout this book. So, you have your price point of how much you want to sell your cupcakes for, now you need to identify who your target market is for the cupcakes. Now I guess you can say that everybody likes cupcakes. Yes and no. Some people like cupcakes, some people don't. But, you can not start your marketing strategy by saying "everybody." You need to be specific because everybody is too wide. I need you to narrow that down so you may say that I'm going to focus these cupcakes on kids. For kid parties or children parties. Now you have a target market for creating cupcakes for children's birthday parties. Now you have a narrower arrow that you can follow. Now, as a part of your marketing strategy, you need to say to yourself, " Hmm, who could I sell these cupcakes to?" Well you can look at dads, you can look at moms, you can look at grandparents. Who's going to buy these cupcakes from you? Who's going to give you those two dollars for that fifty cent cupcake that you're selling? So, who would be most likely to use these cupcakes as it relates to their business. This is another way to think of it. Party planners, event planners, people who actually put together birthday parties for children. So now you begin to identify these are your target markets. These are the people who will be purchasing your cupcakes.

Now I'm going to teach you another term, two in fact. One, B2B, that is business to business, that means, I'm selling my products to your business. So, an example of the cupcake sales, "If I am Cupcake LLC, I am selling cupcakes to Party Event Planner LLC," that would be called B2B, business to business sales. Now, there's another word, B2C, business to consumer sales. Okay, business to consumers is Cupcake LLC is selling those cupcakes Johnny's dad who's planning Johnny's birthday party. Okay, so you have to identify whether or not you are doing B2B (business to business) or B2C (business to consumer) sales. So now the marketing strategy for those two are going to be a little bit different because your marketing material is either going to focus on business owners or consumers. So now you have to identify two levels of marketing presentation that you have to consider. Marketing can be as simple or complex as you need it to be.

Considering you are a small business, considering you are a new business, you still have to look good. You are responsible for being professional and you are responsible for looking good. So, one of the first things that you need to do is create some business cards. Business cards can be very inexpensive. Everyone uses VistaPrint online. You have probably heard the advertisements. You can google business cards and you can find a place that you can use to print out business cards. Business cards are very professional and it can be very simple. You can just put your name on there, a way for them to contact you, an email and a phone number. Put a nice logo on that business card. You can go to an inexpensive resource like Fiverr.com. Those are very cost effective sites where you can go to create business cards, logos and even websites which is another important thing that you have to have in your business.

A website can again be simple or complex. Building your own site has never been easier, especially when you are using a source like GoDaddy.com. There's a lot of different sources that you can go to, again, google it. Build your website, Wix.com is another popular one too as well. Building your website, now you have a web presence. Put that website address on your business card. Now, professionally when you are networking and when you are meeting people, you have that business card, "Yes. I make cupcakes for children's parties. Here's my business card." You have to put yourself out there, networking and marketing is very, very important. So, now, you look good, you have a business card, you know who your target market is, you're speaking about your business now and you are networking.

Another thing that you have to learn how to do is find ways to network. I recommend that you go to Eventbrite.com and look to see in your local area about networking events. Events that allow you to come in, some are for free, some are low cost and some can be expensive. But no matter what it is these are things that you can get yourself out there and market your product. Market your service, market your product, market what you're selling. Because it's one thing to look good with your website, with your business card, with your professional atmosphere that you have as it relates to your presentation of the cupcake craft.

But you also have to make sure that you are getting yourself out there. Nobody wants a secret agent. A secret agent in business is somebody who has a business but nobody knows about it. Why? Because they never talk about it. Don't be a secret agent. Put yourself out there. Tell them what you do. Stand behind your product. Give samples. Give tastings. Do things that are going to allow people to experience everything that you have in that business, especially if it's something that everybody is going to have to have. True enough, everybody eats cupcakes, but you know what, that may be your theme in marketing. Everybody wants a bite of this cupcake. Themes like that are selling points for your business so making sure that you look good is one thing. Making sure that you have a quality product, that is something else.

Don't just get a cereal box recipe. What I mean by cereal box recipe, I mean a recipe that you just poured into a cereal bowl and put some milk in it and say, "Ah, this is my breakfast creation." You could do that because a lot of people have made money by repackaging somebody else's product and selling it to others. But in order to have the competitive edge, you want to do something very special with your product. Instead of having a cereal box type product, be creative. Try new recipes with your cupcakes, with your product. Do things that are going to allow them to want your cupcakes over the other 30,000 other people selling cupcakes. You want to make sure that you are always standing out when it comes to a crowd of competitors. If you were in a room full of cupcake business owners, and everyone is selling cupcakes. You want to make sure that you have the competitive edge to stand out. Maybe your business cards look unique. Maybe your presentation is unique. Maybe the special recipe that you put in that cupcake is unique. No matter what it is in that particular product, you want to make sure that it is very unique. And that you have the competitive edge to sell cupcakes when nobody else can sell cupcakes.

The website is very important for you. I learned this a long time ago. I remember back when I was out of jail and I was starting my business. I looked to different mentors in business to be able to guide my thinking as it relates to creating a successful business. My mentor at the time, and still to this day, I always look in the news to see what she's doing. My girl, Martha Stewart, I mean, I am so proud of her. For her to experience what she's experienced, going to prison and coming out and getting back on top. I really admire her for that alone outside of the other many accomplishments she has achieved. In fact, being a woman with so much creativity and knowledge and just a powerhouse in the business world. I really look up to her because I can appreciate what she brings to the business world. As a woman to go to prison and come back out just as strong. I can appreciate her rigor and her courage to get back on top and to really fight her way to the top.

Martha Stewart has always been one of my heroes in business as I look at my situation and I look at her situation. I got a lot of encouragement from her by just watching the news and reading the news about her story. But one of the things, she wrote a book right after her incarceration. That book was called, "Martha Rules." I remember reading that book and feeling this sense of creativity. I felt encouragement, motivation to jump out there and really go hard in my business. One of the things that she said in this book is, "It is important to make sure you have a website." That was a profound statement back then, because back then websites were not really being done on a day to day basis like you see today in this day in age. Back then, you were special if you had a website. Websites were one of those touchy areas that not everyone had access to a web developer to actually create a website. But at the time, I didn't see the need for a website. But when I read that and she said that a website can help you save time because what you do on that website is you put all the information on there. You put about you, about your company, you put the answers to all of the questions that a person would ask you face to face. You put it all on your website because what that does is strengthen your presentation. It also allows them to go back to that website and refer back to them. You could stand in a room and tell 100 people the same thing and that would tire you out, right? But, if you have a website, and you put it all on there, you can cordially say to someone, "Have you had a chance to check out our website?" Because our website will answer all of those questions. In fact, if you add your name to the mailing list on our website, you will get updates from our company, coupons from our company, and you will have a chance to interact and ask questions that may not have been answered on our website. That was powerful.

That was some powerful information that I got out of that book, Martha Rules. I am saying that the website is important to you because it is part of your marketing piece, it is part of your sales and what you do along with social media. I know a lot of people who say, "Oh, I don't do FaceBook. I don't do twitter." A lot of people say that and the reason being is because of all of the gossip intent that some people have on social media outlets. I use social media outlets to begin to engage new people who may not have access to me. Just because you do not want to participate in the gossip piece of the FaceBooks and Twitters and all these things it is important as a business owner that you get on them. You must conduct yourself in a professional manner as a business owner and get people to engage. This is how you get people to a website. You get people through your twitter and through your facebook. These are people that are not in your community. This is how they get access to you. This is how they hear your story.

Maybe you have a powerful story about how you became a business owner. You were a felon but now you are a business owner. You are now earning an honest living through this business that you started. What an amazing story to put on a social media platform, through an article that you have written; through a blog that you have written. Maybe a video piece that you have recorded, maybe an audio piece you have recorded. However you get your story out, your message, your marketing. This is the message that represents you and this is the thing that allows you to be effective in that world of business growth and business sales. Every moment is an opportunity for sales. Also having an opportunity for those who are not in your community to go online and purchase and order your cupcakes for you to deliver to them or sell to them or ship to them.

However you decide to operate your business and product, I recommend that you have a strong web presence that is allowing you to have access to people who can purchase and buy things from you. These are some of the things on the marketing and sales piece that are very important for you to use to grow your business. With that being said, I hope this information helps to open up some creativity in your mind so that you can begin to do what you need to do to Lockdown the Success in your business. I'm telling you, "We are rolling! I AM SO PROUD OF YOU!" This far in the book we are just over half way there and we are going to make sure that we bring you home because we are determined to help you Lockdown your Success.

Chapter 8:
Building Business Funding and Growing Business Assets

A lot of times when people start their business, they find themselves in a position of needing additional funding. This additional funding is typically used to grow the company. There are so many needs that a new business has and having the finances to operate their new business successfully is very important to them. One of the things that people use new capital for in their new business is to implement their new marketing plan. To be able to hire social media people. To be able to pay for website development, even to purchase business cards needs capital. You have to identify how much capital you need to be able to be in a position to make sure you are fiscally responsible for the amount of capital that you are borrowing. As new business owners you have an opportunity to really grow wealth and assets as it relates to business development. One of the greatest assets that you have in developing your business is the ability to grow financial assets as an entrepreneur.

When I first started my first business, I had no knowledge of this type of process. I had never met anyone such as the wealth planners and portfolio managers that I have met today, that I hadn't met 20 years ago regarding learning how to develop assets in business. I really didn't have this information. I am so excited to share it with you because now you know that this will be an opportunity for you to introduce the wealth management and wealth planners that you will meet in your path. Understand that these people are licensed and they're designed to be able to assist you to grow your wealth. One of the greatest ways to do that is through insurances, policies and different things that their expertise that they can offer to you as a business owner. I mentioned before during the section regarding business operations that risk management is very, very important for you to understand in your new business. Knowing what insurances that have to be in place for your business is very important.

Even down to the type of Errors and Omissions insurance that you have to have.

In order to make sure that your company is operating at a minimum of risk to you as individuals, you want to definitely make sure that you have some type of business insurance. Especially, when you have certain businesses that require you to have different licenses. You definitely want to make sure that as that licensed professional, operating that business, that you are actually insured in the event something was to happen to a client that you are working with or a service that you provided. Errors and Omissions insurance is one of those insurances that help with the liability in the event that someone is going to sue you or accusing you for doing something that you may or may not have done and caused them harm and damages.

Today, I look at myself as more knowledgeable than I did 20 years ago in business. 20 years ago I didn't have anyone to show me exactly what to do and what not to do. I learned a lot of these techniques and strategies just by getting the bruises myself; by having a lot of misfortunes and misinformation. I learned by having a lot of failures in business turned around to my benefit because it allowed me to use those failures, those miscommunications, and misinformation to be able to strengthen me in areas of knowledge that I'm able to share with you today. So when you're building your business you want to make sure you're building the business on a structure that is sound. Part of that sound structure is making sure that you have the revenue flow that you need to be consistently effective and be able to do what you need to do to grow that company.

Sales are a very strong avenue for you to grow wealth in your company. In addition to sales of your products and services you want to look at things long term. Just like you would with your personal finances with a savings account. The same thing as it relates to the business, you want to have a savings account with the business. I know that might sound odd because that's personal and that's business. But it really is not odd because anytime you are doing something that's going to require a set amount of revenue to come out of your company in order for you to get access to a set amount of revenue that will come back into your company. You want to make sure you also have some funding available, sitting there for:

    a) Used to attract more sales to your business
    b) Invest in properly so you can begin to have a return on your investment that's going to also create additional growth in your business and come in as revenue.

Now, as it relates to business funding, a lot of time people look at hard money lending as something to frown on. Who can blame them? Hard money lending is very hard on your finances. It could be if you are not looking at it in an approach that's non-traditional. I'm going to talk to you about the non-traditional approaches of business funding. One of the things that I have done, and I continue to do when I have new projects for my business is, I leverage my personal credit to access business funding. I use this leverage to gain access to funding that will allow me to grow a new business and take it to that next level.

With that particular benefit of having access to that X - amount of dollars there are some drawbacks. The drawbacks are a matter of you assessing your pros and cons. The pros are you typically wouldn't be able to go into a bank or a traditional financial institution and grab this amount of money or funding at the same time because that's just not how the financial situations are set up for you. The other pro is that this allows you to build up your business credit experience so that you can begin to build business credit in your business. It is very important that you have business credit early on in your business. I know that when I started my first company, I set up successful systems to build business credit without knowing that was what I was doing. We had lines of credit. We had credit cards. We had a lot of access to funding for this particular new business. After about five or six years those credit lines would increase. Those credit card limits would increase. I never knew that I would use those because I didn't have a need for them due to the revenue that was coming in so frequently in our company. Five to six years later down the line, there were a couple of things that happened in my business that allowed me to have a need for access to those funds. Thank God that I did have access to those additional funds.

The first thing that happened was that I had an opportunity to become licensed in a particular industry that would allow me to access a higher contract. Now, in order for me to go through the accreditation process for that contract, the accreditation cost me close to $10,000. Had I not gone through the accreditation process, I would not have opened up myself to have access to $100,000 in grants and contracts as it relates to that particular industry. Thank God I had a line of credit. Thank God I had a credit card. Thank God I had access to a savings that we pulled that $10,000 out of to become accredited. That accreditation opened up us to a contract that averaged anywhere from $20,000 to $50,000 a month in revenue. That accreditation increased my business. I was really thankful for forward thinking and having the line of credit along with the credit cards access in my business.

The second thing that happened in my business was, the industry began to change 2 to 3 years down the line and those contracts began to wither down with the changes in the political climate. A lot of people don't realize that as political climates change, meaning republicans to democrats and vice versa, those changes can affect your funding, especially in the nonprofit world. Those things that you were depending on 2 or 3 years ago as it relates to funding coming into your business, you couldn't depend on them the following year because of the political changes that were occurring. What we were able to do as it relates to that was that we were able to sustain our business for years off of the access to funding and credit that we had established with this business. During that time those funds allowed us to keep payroll active, continue to market and create additional sales and it allowed us to go a different direction in our business. The change in direction allowed us to continue to access monthly revenue as frequently as it was before prior to even having access to that bigger contract with that licensing and accreditation. With that being said, you have to really consider the benefits of having access to funding all at one time and being able to use that to grow your business.

On the other hand, the cons to this kind of funding is typically the success fees assessed on this type of funding are costly. The average success fee can be anywhere between 20% to 25% of the funding that you access. Just to give you a quick run down on the math of these nontraditional sources of hard money lending will get you access, lets just say to $100,000 worth of funding. Well, 20% to 25% has to go back to them out of this funding for their fees for their service because they are consulting and they are working on your behalf to access this cash. There's typically a team of people that are working on your behalf to get you access to this funding. They are putting together business profiles and marketing tools, and strategies to be able to allow you to have access to this type of funding. They are working on your behalf. Success fee just means that they do not get paid until you get paid. Meaning until you access the funding they do not get paid a fee from you. The success fee is really serving two purposes. One, they are working for free on your behalf to get access to funding for your business. Number two, they are only getting paid after the fact based on their work performance and the amount of funding they were able to get for you. If they are not able to get you anything, then you are giving 20% to 25% of nothing. If they are able to get you $100,000 then you are giving 20% ($20,000) to 25% ($25,000) out of that. The other con of that is yes you have that amount missing out of your bank but imagine what you can do in your business with $75,000.

Any savvy business person knows that in order to get to where you need to be, you have to make sacrifices. If that sacrifice is paying a high fee for the amount of funding that you have been given access to then you have to evaluate the value. Evaluation has to be made on a case by case basis. For me in many, many cases it has been worth it in starting a successful business. So, I recommend that if you are looking to take your business to a level of increased profit margin but need the funding to be able to do that. It is very wise for you to evaluate the opportunity to use these funding sources that we are talking about as it relates to hard money lending.

Another thing that I would like to highlight as it relates to building business funds for your business. I mentioned earlier that it is important that you take the funding and you do things that are going to create other revenue for you. Of course you have your sales of your products and services that are going to create revenue for you. You also need to look at investments. What can you do with that dollar, the access to the funds that you have that can be used to invest and create additional revenue out of there.

Now, I will tell you a little story about myself and how I came to meet people in the financial services world that benefited me greatly in business. About 10 or 15 years ago, one of my former classmates from undergrad college introduced himself to me. He mentioned to me that he worked for a financial institution that specializes in providing insurance for individuals. Now when I hear insurance, in my mind I think okay when I die, then I benefit. That doesn't make sense. How can I die and benefit? Well, if I die and I have a life insurance policy on me and I leave that money to my kids then I do not benefit. He said, "No, no, no. This is something that will allow you to reap the benefits while you are still alive." He said something very, very, important to me, and it changed my life. He said, "Life insurance is the greatest transfer of wealth." I asked him, "What do you mean by that?" What he meant by that is when you have access to people in your life that know the financial world like they do, be sure to soak in that information and apply it to everything that you do. Did I get that out of that one sentence? No. I got that out of sitting by his feet, literally, and learning as much as I could learn about how financial products can be used to my advantage when it comes to business development and growing assets for the business.

When I had a chance to do that, I had an opportunity to look at options for growing the assets in my business. So what I did in that instance, I took what he said and I broke it down. I broke it down to pieces in my mind. So if insurance is the greatest transfer of wealth then we have to look at what we are insuring. And I asked him the question, "What are we insuring?" One of the things that he spoke to me about was annuities. He spoke to me about being able to have products in place that in the event that I was to become disabled, then I would still have access to finances to be able to provide for my care. Okay, that's fine. But that's another situation of misfortune that I would be in. So talking to me about the benefits of being able to have access to funding while I'm still living.

Then we began to have a story and a conversation discussion regarding how we can take that information and apply it to my business? He began to run what they call illustrations in the financial world. He would show me some of my illustrations based off of my age, my health and if I was a nonsmoker vs. smoker. I began to look at these illustrations. I am going to share a little bit about the illustrations that I had from him and what I began to participate in. I saw an opportunity where I could have a policy based off of my age and health at the time where I would actually contribute to. The craziest thing about this policy is, I looked those illustrations and those numbers and I couldn't believe what I was seeing. Basically I had a policy for $250,000 of whole life and I paid $1800 a month over a 5 year period and on the 6th I would have access to a line of credit of what I had contributed. It was amazing to see those numbers.

Just to know that these particular products exist was really life changing. Now, with this new information, I could build wealth based off of accessing these policies to grow my company and increase my net worth. What is Net Worth? According to investopedia, "Net worth is the amount by which assets exceed liabilities. Another way to say this is, it's the value of everything you own, minus all your debts. Net Worth is a concept that can be applied to both individuals and businesses, as a measure of how much they are really worth." Imagine that, a felon with a net worth. I would never imagine in a million years, me as a felon would have a net worth. I mean, even just saying that today. I have two felonies but I also have a strong net worth. Your net worth, I learned earlier on from people in this profession, that we have to set a goal for ourselves. I remember the first time that I sat down with him. He asked me, he said, "How much do you want to be worth?" I didn't know how to answer that question. The first answer that came to my mind about that was, I want to be worth a lot. He said, "Okay, I get that, I'm sure you want to be worth a lot. Everybody wants to be worth a lot. Give me a number that you want to be worth." Meaning, how much do I want to have access to a month when I retire. So, I thought about that. Then, I said, "Well, you know what, I want to be worth, hmm, $100,000 a month."

Okay, so he began to set a plan for me based off of these financial products that would allow me to have a lifestyle. A lifestyle that would give me the benefit of living off of $100,000 a month tax free. Amazing! Once we hit that goal, we went higher. We went higher and we went higher. And I learned how to use those goals to apply it to not just one of my businesses but to a multiple range of businesses. Back when we got to talking about Key-Man policies, Partnerships, and Buy-Sell agreements. All of these things that businesses do not have in place because they are not knowledgeable or in the KNOW that these products exist. You would be amazed by the amount of business owners that do not know about this and the amount of people in the financial world who are trying to interact with people like you and me to show them that this is a way of growing wealth. My recommendation to you is to continue to seek knowledge always in your business. Continue seeking knowledge especially when it comes to the financial management of your business. This is how you grow assets in your business.

When you have assets sitting on your company, a $250,000 asset, okay. Don't look at that premium that you are paying every month, $1,800 a month, as a liability. But look at the asset that it's creating. I don't mind creating a liability in my business as long as it's going to create an asset. Because I know from those assets, I am able to leverage lines of credit that are going to allow me to really have access to my own personal banks. I will have created my own personal bank when it comes to accessing those assets to create a new company or to grow an existing company that I have. Being able to know that is very, very important.

Now I am not a licensed person, so I can't give you advice. I am telling you about me. I am saying to you that it's important that you seek out the knowledge of a licensed professional that will be able to talk to you about insurances, asset building and even asset protection. I recommend that you consult with an attorney knowledgeable in business practices that will help you identify ways to protect the assets that you are growing. Some of your best friends in business should be one, your attorney. Two, it should be your financial portfolio manager, those who are able to grow your assets. And number three it should be your business consultant. Number four, it should also be your funding partner. Funding partner, meaning those people who give you access to hard money lending. Those four people on your team create some of the things that help you lockdown success.

I mean as a felon, I think it's pretty good that you can actually put yourself in position to grow wealth. I mean, through business development I believe this is one of the ways that you can get to this next level and really make an impact, not only in your own lives but in the people around you. Just because you have gained the knowledge and have the ability now, to share it with others. Success Lockdown is about locking down your success not just mentally but also financially. Because once you are able to lock it down mentally and financially, you are able to make an impact in the lives of other people as it relates to the Success Lockdown. From me to you, I want you to be successful. I want you to have access to this information sooner than later. Had I known this information 20 years ago, I would have been further along in life than I am now. I want you to get further than me.

I remember what my mentor, Dr. Tina, told me, she said, "A great mentor always wants their mentee to rise higher than they have ever been." That's one of the things that I have kept with me, over and over life long. I believe that it is important that I become responsible for imparting what I have to others just like you. That is why writing this book has been very important for me. Getting this information out to you has been just as important. I need you to Lockdown Success so that you can represent other felons that need to see people like me and you out there locking down success just like we have done it. It's not impossible. In fact it's mandatory that you succeed. I was talking to a friend this morning and we were just motivating each other. We were getting each other pumped up with what we need to do for the new year and what we need to do bigger as it relates to business development. One of the things that she said to me which I really, really enjoy, and I take it to heart because of what she said. "Failure is not an option, we cannot fail. I say to you, "When it comes to locking down success, you have to get it in your mind that FAILURE IS NOT AN OPTION! We have already been beat down! We have felonies! We have already taken a loss! Now it's time to walk into our gain! Our gain is the information we need to Lockdown our Success TODAY!"

Chapter 9:
The Importance of Self Promotion and Networking in Business

One of the hardest things that I have had to deal with in business development is self-development. It's not easy to self-promote or talk about myself. It has never been easy for me. I am very proud of my accomplishments as an entrepreneur. I am very proud of what I have done academically. What I am most proud of is how I carry myself amongst those who have not had the background I have had. What I mean by that is. In the business world you will meet all types of people. You meet people who come from a family of business. The other day I was at a Jewelry store looking at some jewelry and I stopped in the store and I had a talk with the sales gentleman. It didn't take long before I realized I was talking to one of the store owners of a chain of jewelry stores here in the Tampa Bay area. What I learned from this gentleman is that this store had been in the family for over 40 years. I learned that they came to this country over 40 years ago to capture the American dream. He said that his family came because they wanted to have a better way of life. He said that entrepreneurship came naturally to them as a family. Back home where they are from they had to work hard for everything they did. Once they got here, their work ethic never changed up.

Speaking with him, he said that in the jewelry business that they take pride in what they do. They learned as much as they could about diamonds and they actually learned about their community because they wanted to be able to have a community connection that was going to be lasting. They have been known for making customized jewelry for football players and other celebrities that come through. But out of all of the things that we spoke about the other night, the thing that stuck out in my head was that their sense of pride in what they do and in their business has been in their family for years. That is the legacy. Their legacy is making sure that they produce a quality product. The second part of their legacy is making sure that they interact with people and the community in a way that allows people to trust them. To really become a source for standing behind their product and having people recommend their products and services to others. That's how they have built their relationships in the community and their customer base. They have put in the necessary time to get to know who comes in and out of their store. It was no wonder that I spent an hour or more just talking with this gentleman.

I asked him what type of marketing they do. I am always intrigued by how business owners market themselves. They said that they don't really do a lot of marketing. He said that their marketing is when they interact with people every day. Their marketing is their level of professionalism and their knowledge base of their product and how they relate to people. I really enjoyed this conversation with this gentleman. I felt proud of them. I told him that I was proud of them. I also told him that his interaction with me made me feel so comfortable because I felt like he could relate to me in so many ways. So, when I think about people like him and how they self promote and how they spend time to connect with people. There has to be a recipe there for success. Of course they're successful. They have store chains all over the area, maybe 5, 6, or 7 more stores. Right there in the mall as well. As I think about them, it allows me to think about others who take their brand to that next level by the way that they self promote. I think back about how with some people like them, self promotions is easy. First and foremost because they are proud of where they came from.

How do you self promote when you are not so proud of where you came from? Sure I have a degree, or 2 or 3 maybe 4 but sometimes there's a hesitation in my voice, always, almost always when I remind myself that I have felonies. How do I get rid of this badge of shame? And I have to ask myself, do I get rid of this badge of shame? It's becoming part of my make up. I put on these felonies when I wake up in the morning. I almost try to take them off before I go to bed each night. So that I can dream about the impossible throughout the night. As I am dreaming about the impossible, I wake up with more opportunity, more rigor, more motivation for the day ahead because I have to work ten times harder than the next person, not just in business but in life. Because I have a badge of shame that I have to deal with.

So, how do I deal with it Dr. Brown? Dr. Brown with the felony. Dr. Brown with the marks against her. How do I deal with it? I deal with it every day. I deal with it with prayer. I deal with it with transparency. I deal with is with self evaluation. I deal with it with a mindset that just because I have a felony doesn't mean the felony has me. Just because I have 2 felonies, those 2 felonies don't have me. Because what I have, is motivation. If you strip away the degrees, you still have motivation. You have to know that no matter what you are dealing with, this badge of shame should not hold you down from your potential of being everything that God put in you to be.

You have that right to live. You have that right to be successful. You have that right to grow. Don't let nobody take that right from you. Don't let nobody make you compromise what you can be. Don't ever let nobody take away or add to you. Don't ever let nobody put shame in your path. Because I commission you to take that shame and turn it into victory. Why? Because they deserve it. Those lives that you have not met yet that you will touch. They deserve it! Most importantly, YOU DESERVE IT! YOU deserve that chance to grow beyond your capacity. YOU deserve that opportunity to engage with a person without shame. And add a Badge of Honor that you have made the proper steps to change your life. YOU have made the proper steps to advance past your blemishes and your criminal background.

"You are the captain of your soul", as the great author William Ernest Henley once wrote. "It is written: 'Man shall not live on bread alone, but on every word that comes from the mouth of God." Matthew 4:4 It is written and it is written well. I take those words with me almost everyday. Because if it wasn't for the bread and the Word of God, I would not have the courage to speak about the blemishes, the shame, the badge. I want you to think about this. I want you to really allow this to soak into your mind. You don't owe anybody a damn thing from this point forward. But what you do owe them is a chance to get to know

YOU and to learn about everything that you have been through up until this point that led you to believe that you too can walk into the world of entrepreneurship.

See, I believe in you. I believe in your ability to sell yourself to yourself. Before you can sell yourself to anybody else with a felony, you have to sell yourself to yourself. It took many years to sell myself to myself. Why? Because I don't self promote, that's not my character. I have always been a behind the scenes person. Even when I'm in business and I'm placed in the front, I fall to the back because I'm content to be a worker bee. I'm content to serve. But today I am content to serve in a different capacity. I'm okay with serving you as the author of this book. Why? Because, again, I am looking forward to changing the lives of the people I have yet to meet.

I hope that as you read this book, you begin to receive some enlightenment. It's a removal of guilt. It's a removal of responsibility. The responsibility of letting yourself off the hook. You have done your time. You have paid your debt. You may be reading this and your are paying your debt right now. Whether it be finishing up your jail time sentence or your probation. I don't care if you were in prison 20 years ago or more just like I have experienced. One of the best ways you will succeed in business is learning how to carry your badge. And your badge is this, self promotion is okay.

Being proud of yourself is okay. Being successful is okay. I don't know how many times a week I have to tell myself, "It's okay to be successful. IT'S OKAY TO BE SUCCESSFUL!" I want you to practice telling yourself, "IT IS OKAY TO BE SUCCESSFUL! IT IS OKAY TO LOCKDOWN SUCCESS!" I want you to begin to tell yourself that everyday. Look in the mirror, stand tall, you speak to yourself in that mirror and you tell yourself that , "IT IS OKAY TO BE SUCCESSFUL!" Sometimes when I am looking in the mirror, I don't recognize that other person in front of me. Of course it could be the weight loss I have experienced over the last few months. I don't recognize myself sometimes. I don't think it's just the weight loss though. I think who I recognize isn't that person 20 years ago. It's the person that I stand before boldly, with confidence and self love. I had to learn how to love myself again. I had to learn how to believe in myself again.

I was just a baby when I caught those charges. I was a little bitty girl in my mind. I had yet to understand what the world was about to do to me. I had no understanding about what God was about to do for me. I couldn't imagine the doors that would open 20 years later. I couldn't even imagine what my 20 years would look like because of those criminal charges at the time. Looking back, I see that those things changed me. Looking forward I know that those things changed me for the better. In my business, I get a chance to speak about my past. I get a chance to self promote now. I get a chance to interact and engage with other entrepreneurs and potential entrepreneurs. I get to tell them that 20 years ago I served time. I was convicted. I get a chance to be transparent and self promote. I can tell them that just because I did something 20 years ago, I'm not going to let that dictate something for the rest of my life.

With all of that being said, I say to you, "In order to have a successful business, you have to gauge your audience, interact with others, you have to network. But before you walk into that door to network, I want you to be 100% clear on something. YOU DESERVE TO BE IN THAT ROOM! I remember when I first started my business and I began to attend networking events. I would go in there and I would see people dressed professionally, speaking professionally, acting professionally. I didn't feel like I fit in. I felt like I was the only one in the room with a felony. Maybe I was, maybe I wasn't. But you know what? That didn't matter! I had to go in and I had to self promote! I had to talk about my service and my products to strangers without feeling like I had to run out of the room. As I would speak to them, I shared my heart about my services and my product every single time. Why? Because when you are quiet about what you do, your sales for that week are going to be quiet about what they do for your bank account. I laugh, but I am so serious with you.

You can NOT be a secret agent, I can't stress that enough over and over again. My sister is a licensed Real Estate Agent. She taught me that term a couple of years ago when she first graduated. She said that they said, "You have to tell everybody what you do in order to build up your database of people to get to know." So, you can't be a secret agent when it comes to disclosing to others that you are a Real Estate Agent. You never know where your next sale or closing is going to be. So you have to keep your business cards on you, they taught her. And you have to make sure that you tell everybody and their mama, licensed realtor that's how you get the sale. That's how you get the interest. Connect with people. So just like a brand new realtor, I want you to self promote. I want you to have your business cards on you at all times. Don't ever get caught without your business cards on you. Never miss an opportunity to self promote, network and engage. Go to Eventbrite and try to find local networking events. Because when you discover local networking events, you will find that many of them meet monthly. You go in there and you meet people. You may run into somebody just like you. Sure, I'm not saying wear your felony on your sleeve, but I do want you to be aware that just because you have felonies doesn't mean you're the only one in the room with a felony. I want you to be less self conscious of these badges.

You have to put on new badges and begin to exchange those negative badges for positive badges. Positive badges that speak to your character. Things like integrity, things like social ability, things like characteristics. Look at these words and find how these words can contribute to your success and your growth of your business and everything you are putting in it to grow it. You have to be responsible for self promotion. Sure you could hire a marketing company, but guess what? You are still going to have to self promote to that marketing company. If you can't find something positive to say about yourself, guess what? I want you to cheat. I want you to ask someone very close to you, someone that's a supporter of you, someone that loves you, someone that is there for you. Ask them to be honest with you. Ask them to give you three words that describe you. Tell them don't do it out of love, tell them don't do it out of support, don't do it because you need to hear something positive. I want you to tell them to do it because it's what they believe to be true about you. Tell them you need them to do it because they are part of your process for Locking down Success.

Chapter 10:
Success Lockdown

I have a secret, "I'm afraid of the dark." I wasn't always afraid of the dark. Circumstances in my early years allowed me to be put in a place where the dark and the unknown became very foreign to my path and my direction. My secret is not a secret for those who have walked in my shoes. What people don't understand about those who have been incarcerated is, our fear of the darkness has to do with our fear of the unknown. See, what happens is, the minute that we are incarcerated we know instantly that our freedom is taken, our rights are removed, our ability to be is held in the hands of those to whom we have been placed into the custody of.

Being in the custody of the jail, the prison system, the penal system, we know then that justice somehow has failed us. It doesn't mean we don't acknowledge what we have done. When I say we, I'm talking about us felons. I know what I did, I also know what I didn't do. I know that there are times when I am guilty as hell. Then there are times when I am just as innocent. Where was I guilty? I was guilty the day I went into the police department under custody for my crime. And they told me to just give them a statement, then I could get ready and go home. That was a lie. Somebody lied to me. That was the first time that the justice system, the penal system lied to me.

They didn't tell me that I should have not said anything until a lawyer came and sat with me. No one encouraged me to know my rights. No one told me, "If you ever get in trouble, and they take you into custody, the first thing you do is remain silent until you have the legal representation of an attorney. I was scared, I just wanted to go home. I didn't know that one mistake would cost me ten years of my life. I didn't know that one mistake would cause me 20 years or more later to have dreams of being scared of the dark. But what I feel guilty of is just like no other group of people. Those who do things and then say another,

"Guilty as Charged." There are many ways that I am innocent. I was a baby when this happened. I didn't know what I was doing. I didn't know that, that one mistake of not having an attorney being present during my questioning could interrupt the rest of my case and prevent me from really going home that day.

I say all of that to say this to you. Your fears become your strengths mentally if you allow them to be. I had to embrace the darkness. I had to embrace the unknown. I had to realize that, at the end of the day, we are not in control when they take our freedom. They take more than our freedom. They take our hope, they take our existence in life. They take our dreams. I remember sitting in that jail cell. Trying to get some understanding about where would I be other than sitting in this jail cell? What would my parents think? What would my family think? What would my friends think? I never stopped to evaluate what I was thinking. All I know is that I felt like the end was near.

What I didn't realize was, life for me was just beginning. I want to make sure that you understand that Success Lockdown is NOT just about business. It's about freedom. It's about the ability to take the unknown and be in the KNOW. Being the movement of knowledge. When you look in the mirror, you see one thing, you see that person with the felon. But you also see that person who survived. You see that person that wants something better than what they had in the past. I mean of course you can look in the mirror, you could see the image you hate, you could see the image of disappointment, you can see the image of hurt, but you have to make a conscious choice to change that imagery of what you see when you look in the mirror.

It took me twenty years to look in the mirror. I haven't looked in a mirror in 20 years. I was ashamed of my past. I didn't want to talk about it. I didn't want to experience it. I didn't want to feel like that again. I didn't want to address it. I didn't want to write a book that was going to continuously remind me of that horrible experience that I experienced back in 1996. I didn't want to have a book that was a reminder of the hurt that I see when I look into my mother's eyes and I say, "It's been a long time since I have been in the KNOW of what happened to me when I went to jail.

On another note, I want you to realize that being afraid of the dark, doesn't mean that you don't do anything. The darkness could be like, all you have to do is close your eyes. Remember that canvas we talked about early on in the book? It's your opportunity to paint that canvas now. See, the Success Lockdown has everything to do with you and nothing to do with that justice or that penal system that you experienced pain in. No, the Success Lockdown is an opportunity for you to face your fears head on.

As I write this book, I think about how things are becoming so surreal to me. Prior to writing this last chapter, I sat down with my publicist. It was such a humbling experience for me, to tell this wonderful stranger everything that happened to me while I was in jail. Only for her to look back at me and to tell me about my strengths. She told me about my ability to impact lives. She told me about my abilities to use this book as a platform to speak to others in my situation, out of my situation and those who will be going into my situation of incarceration. She said that when they get out, they will have a plan. That plan is the Success Lockdown. I took a step back because, just like any good publicist, they impart into you the rigor of information that encourages you to keep talking. To keep speaking about your situation. Believing that your situation was just a situation of trial but it was a situation of triumph.

I'm very humbled by the amount of hands that have put their hands on this project because they believe in the Success Lockdown. You locking down your success is so important to me because I know what it's like to feel abandoned, hurt and ashamed and not have any resources to help me to rise above any of those feelings. I remember a time in my life when I would see opportunities and think they are failures if I don't pursue them. Sometimes I realize that not every opportunity is for you to pursue.

Everything is on God's timing and when we take our time and do things on God's timing that's one of the best flows of life you can experience as an individual. I am thankful that God has imparted in me the tools that I can give to you as resources in this book. There are six things I want to highlight to you. That I believe it's important for you to really see all of the way through for the Success Lockdown.

1. **Be proud of yourself.** I mean it, You have to be proud of yourself because no one is going to be responsible for being more proud than you about you. Being proud of yourself helps you to build the momentum you need to go forward.
2. **Don't apologize for wanting to be successful.** Many people tend to regret success because once they achieve it, they may have feelings of resentment from those who have not yet challenged themselves enough to achieve it. You have to learn how to celebrate the milestones of your success in a way that offers value for your own accomplishments.
3. **Identify your barriers To success.** You have to develop a mechanism for self-evaluation in a way that it becomes automated and integrated into a process for forward thinking. Never let family, friends, or close associates deter your ability to go in a direction that fosters growth and credibility.
4. **Create a muse for what your success should look like.** My muse for life is similar to my muse for business development. You have to find a wave of inspiration in your wind of motivation to succeed. As many times as you may want to quit, you have to explore the many ways in which you have to keep going. Your muse should be specific to your cause and your cause should mimic your mission.
5. **Find a success model to mirror.** When you look in the mirror, facing yourself can be a humbling experience. If there is any blame for making a mess at life, you will always get the finger pointed at you. Your model that you mirror can come from any walk of life that you could relate to. Success is not promised. The rational promise to make should be associated with connecting with the right person that can be the midwife for your goals. Dream again and this time do so in color.

6. **Always push yourself beyond your capacity.** You have to be responsible for creating the best you that the world has ever known. Push yourself like a world class boxer, treat yourself like a champion. Be aware of what is going on around you at all times as you stretch your territory. The best push in life will come from a place inside you that speaks to you in riddles but produces like well written poetry. Exceed your personal expectations of yourself as often as possible.

www.ingramcontent.com/pod-product-compliance
Lightning Source LLC
Chambersburg PA
CBHW071911070526
44583CB00016B/1939